Rewiring Your Mind for AI

**How to Think, Work, and Thrive
in the Age of Intelligence**

David A. Wood, Ph.D.

Technics Publications
SEDONA, ARIZONA

TECHNICS PUBLICATIONS

115 Linda Vista, Sedona, AZ 86336 USA
https://www.TechnicsPub.com

Edited by Steve Hoberman
Cover design by Lorena Molinari

First Printing 2025

ISBN, print ed.9781634627566
ISBN, Kindle ed.9781634627573
ISBN, PDF ed.9781634627580

Library of Congress Control Number: 2025936419

For God, Cindy, Jessica and Bryce, Bryan, Derek, and Emily.
For my parents and my in-laws.
I love and thank you all!

Contents

Introduction: Thriving an AI-Driven World _____ 1

Chapter 1: Behind the Curtain: How AI Works_____ 17

Chapter 2: AI is Not a Calculator _____ 27

Chapter 3: It's *Not* Google_____ 41

Chapter 4: Using GenAI is Cheating_____ 51

Chapter 5: When Beginners do the Impossible _____ 65

Chapter 6: Learning will Never be the Same _____ 79

Chapter 7: Becoming an AI-Centaur _____ 95

Chapter 8: Perfect is the Enemy of Good_____ 111

Chapter 9: The Hidden Bias in AI_____ 125

Chapter 10: AI Gone Wrong _____ 133

Chapter 11: Changing and Sustaining New AI Mindsets __ 147

Chapter 12: Managing AI and Humans _____ 157

Conclusion: Your Move_____ 173

Index _____ 181

Thriving in an AI-Driven World: The Power of Mindset

When the first calculators became widely available in the 1960s, people didn't rush to celebrate. Instead, they worried. Students, businesspeople, and even engineers feared these new devices might make people lazy or ruin their ability to do even basic arithmetic. In some circles, using a calculator felt like cheating. But, over time, the stigma faded, and calculators were embraced. Rather than destroying our mathematical abilities, they transformed them, allowing us to focus on solving bigger and more creative problems.

Today, we're seeing the same story play out, but on a much larger scale, with artificial intelligence, or AI. AI isn't just another tool in our toolbox—it's something far more disruptive. It's a technology that forces us to rethink not only how we work but also how we think about our own capabilities. And just like the adoption of calculators, how we respond to AI depends entirely on our mindset.

Mindsets are powerful. They shape how we see the world, how we act, and even how we solve problems. Take my mother-in-law, for example. She's a person who, like each of us, was shaped by her choices, the world around her, and her life experiences. Born in 1956, she spent most of her life before the Internet became widespread. Her way of thinking was shaped in a "pre-Internet" world. Every once in a while you can see how that shapes her approach to solving problems today. For instance, occasionally, she will call my wife with a question, like "What can I use to remove an ink stain?" or "What channel is the BYU football game on?" My wife listens patiently and then says, "Mom, just Google it." My mother-in-law will laugh and reply, "I didn't even think about that."

My mom grew up during a similar time. My mom's great at Googling things, and texting, but rarely makes a "long-distance" phone call. When my mom grew up, making long-distance phone calls was very expensive. Money was tight in her family and so long-distance calls were reserved for very special occasions or emergencies, and the calls were short. This made sense when you had to pay for long-distance calls.

That mindset about long-distance calls still influences my mom, even though technology has changed. Phone companies no longer charge you by the minute for long-distance calls. Long-distance calls are essentially free once you pay for a basic phone service. My mom knows and understands this, her mindset still prevents her from acting on it. We have told her numerous times, "Why don't you just call your grandkids and chat with them?" She invariably responds, just like my mother-in-law, "I didn't even think of that!" Even though my mom is great at texting her grandkids, the mindset that long-distance phone calls are expensive—and therefore should be limited—continues to govern her behavior, long after it's relevant to the current reality.

For both women, their mindsets about what they can and can't do still affect their lives. Now, neither of these are major concerns, because an extra phone call to ask how to do something or not thinking to call your grandkids has limited effect. In other cases, our mindsets can have much larger impacts on our lives.

History is full of examples where mindsets determined outcomes. To illustrate how quickly adapting—or clinging—to old ways of thinking can influence results, consider these brief examples.

In the corporate world, success often goes to those who reinvent themselves. For example, Nokia—once a global mobile leader—hesitated to move beyond hardware-centric phones, and its reluctance to embrace the smartphone revolution ultimately cost it dearly. In contrast, IBM, on the brink of collapse in the early '90s, transformed itself by pivoting from mainframes to integrated services. Tesla's bold bet on electric vehicles upended established automakers, forcing them to overhaul their product lines. Airbnb's radical home-sharing concept challenged traditional hotels and reshaped the travel landscape.

Innovation is relentless, and those who fail to evolve are left behind. The shift from horse-drawn carriages to automobiles wasn't just about new machines; companies like Studebaker retooled their entire identity to build cars, while others clung to the old ways and vanished. During the Industrial Revolution, the Luddites fiercely resisted mechanized textile equipment even as progress marched on, a stark reminder that resistance to change can be self-defeating. When the world of reference material moved online, the venerable Encyclopedia Britannica lost ground to the dynamic, crowdsourced Wikipedia, demonstrating that static institutions must adapt or be replaced.

Political leadership has long depended on the ability to connect with the public, and mindset shifts here have reshaped history. U.S. President Franklin D. Roosevelt's fireside chats via radio brought comfort and clarity during the Great Depression, while John F. Kennedy's masterful performance in the first televised presidential debates redefined political communication. John McCain, the late U.S. Senator and presidential candidate, famously admitted in 2008 that he didn't know how to use a computer or send an email. This wasn't a big deal earlier in his career, but during his presidential campaign, it symbolized a broader disconnect with the digital world. Barack Obama, by contrast, embraced social media and digital technology, using platforms like Twitter (now X) and Facebook to energize younger voters. This mindset difference helped Obama connect with a tech-savvy electorate and win the presidency, while McCain's hesitation became a point of criticism and contributed to his loss.

In the world of sports, new ideas often rewrite the record books. LeBron James is one of the most decorated basketball players in NBA history. While his on-court performance is remarkable, his dedication to taking care of his body sets him apart from many other athletes. You can read stories of past NBA greats like Larry Bird, who had a legendary work ethic but lacked discipline in nutrition—he was known to eat entire wedding cakes by himself. Magic Johnson's career was cut short after contracting HIV due to his promiscuous, risky lifestyle choices. Meanwhile, Michael Jordan and Wilt Chamberlain regularly smoked cigars or cigarettes, habits that did not enhance their health.

In contrast to these all-time greats, LeBron has a health mindset that is superior to other superstars. His adoption of high-tech monitoring tools, detailed performance metrics, and recovery strategies has allowed him to adjust his game continuously, setting a new standard for longevity in professional sports. At age 40, he is still performing as one of the top players in the NBA, while reportedly spending approximately $1.5 million a year to maintain his health.

Some of the greatest leaps in human progress have come from challenging deeply held mindsets. Early in medicine, the widespread rejection of germ theory delayed life-saving practices until pioneers like Semmelweis, Pasteur, and Lister forced the establishment to reckon with evidence, ultimately transforming healthcare. The genomics revolution—once an expensive, arcane science—is now paving the way for personalized medicine, and it happened because researchers dared to challenge established limits.

Cultural industries are perhaps the most visible battlegrounds for mindset shifts. The film world's abrupt transition from silent movies to "talkies" forced actors and directors to reinvent their craft overnight, while the music industry's move from CDs to digital streaming upended decades of physical media dominance. Television has been transformed by on-demand streaming platforms that bypass traditional cable and theatrical models, and comic books have reinvented themselves as cinematic universes. The fashion industry now finds its creative process influenced by social media and real-time consumer feedback, which is a complete reversal of the old top-down mindset that the people at the top knew better than the customers.

Each of these rapid-fire examples—from corporate turnarounds and technological revolutions to political reimagining, athletic breakthroughs, scientific paradigm shifts, and cultural reinventions—demonstrates that mindsets are central to success and failure. Clinging to outdated mindsets can leave individuals, companies, and even entire societies trailing behind. As technology continues to evolve at an unprecedented pace, the ability to challenge and reframe our mental models will be essential—not only for survival but for thriving in a rapidly changing world.

Mindsets don't just affect business executives, politicians, sports stars, and grandmas. Mindsets affect each of us in all aspects of our lives. Clearly mindsets are important, but what exactly are they?

A mindset refers to the established set of attitudes, beliefs, and assumptions that an individual holds about themselves, others, and the world.

It shapes how a person interprets and responds to situations, challenges, and opportunities. Mindsets influence behavior, decision-making, and the willingness to learn, adapt, and grow.

A tremendous amount has been written and said about mindsets. This book is not about all mindsets, or even necessarily the most important mindsets. Rather, I aim to discuss how mindsets, especially of working professionals, need to change given the tremendous rise of AI. Since the release of ChatGPT 3.5 by OpenAI in November of 2022, I have focused my academic research, teaching, consulting, and personal time on this amazing technology. Across all these endeavors, I have realized the need most of us have to update our mindset for the "new AI world" that exists because of easily accessible AI. Just like my mother-in-law needs to realize that "Googling it" is available and my mom needs to adjust her thinking about long-distance phone calls, all of us need to realize that to be successful in this AI world we need to adjust our mindsets.

Before we jump into the specific mindsets that we should update or create, I want to talk about the idea of two more general mindsets, a growth mindset versus a fixed mindset. Dr. Carol Dweck is a psychologist known for her work on motivation and learning. She introduced the concept of fixed versus growth mindsets, which describe how people perceive their abilities. A fixed mindset assumes that intelligence and talent are static traits, leading individuals to avoid challenges and fear failure. With a fixed mindset, you are what you are, and you can't change.

In contrast, a growth mindset embraces the idea that you can develop abilities through effort, learning, and perseverance. With a growth mindset, personal growth is unlimited. You can become whatever and whoever you want to become. The growth mindset encourages resilience, a love for learning, and a willingness to take on challenges. The following table summarizes the differences between a growth and a fixed mindset.

Fixed Mindset	Growth Mindset
Believes intelligence, talent, and abilities are fixed and cannot be changed.	Believes intelligence, talent, and abilities can be developed through effort and learning.
Avoids challenges for fear of failure.	Embraces challenges as opportunities to grow.
Gives up easily when faced with obstacles.	Persists through obstacles and learns from failures.
Views effort as pointless ("If I'm not good at it, I never will be").	Views effort as the path to mastery.
Feels threatened by the success of others.	Feels inspired and motivated by others' success.
Takes criticism personally.	Uses feedback to improve.

This book builds on the idea that we can change our mindsets. We can all have a growth mindset. This is critically important because the changes that are coming to us individually, to our businesses, and to our society because of AI will be transformative. With a growth mindset, we will be prepared for this exciting future.

With a fixed mindset, we will be in big trouble.

You might be thinking, AI is just hype! Maybe you have even tried it and found that it didn't work in the way you hoped. Perhaps your initial impressions were right, or perhaps more experimenting would be useful. The more I use AI, the more convinced I am that this is going to be as transformative as the Internet, the computer, and maybe even electricity. Why am I so bullish about this technology? Let me give you a few examples, to encourage you to consider changing your mindset about AI from a fixed mindset to a growth mindset.

Let's start with hype. Overhyped tech gets praised for what it *might* do someday—not what it is actually doing right now. Technology that is not overhyped can accomplish meaningful tasks right now. Generative AI is already powering real change in everyday tasks across diverse fields. Consider, for example, what happened when Italy banned ChatGPT on April 1, 2023, for all citizens of the country. Italy issued the ban just a few months after the release of ChatGPT 3.5 and not long after the release of ChatGPT 4. Researchers found that even though ChatGPT technology was new, the programming productivity of approximately 8,000

Italian coders dropped by about 50%. The demand for ChatGPT was so high that after only two days, there was a spike in downloads of virtual private networks (VPNs), technology that would allow Italian programmers to access ChatGPT from other countries.

Let's move to an example from Amazon.com. In the second quarter earnings call in 2024, Amazon CEO Andy Jassy highlighted how the company's AI-driven coding assistant, Q Developer, has significantly accelerated software modernization. With its code transformation capabilities, Amazon successfully migrated 30,000 product applications from older Java versions (Java 8 or 11) to Java 17. This shift has resulted in substantial efficiency gains, saving the company an estimated 4,500 *years* of development work and reducing costs by approximately $260 million annually through performance improvements.

Now, look to Hollywood, where AI-driven technology is reshaping the way films and television shows are made. A prime example is Disney's very popular *The Mandalorian*, which revolutionized production through StageCraft, an advanced virtual filmmaking system. StageCraft employs massive LED walls that display real-time, AI-assisted, computer-generated environments. This allows filmmakers to dynamically adjust lighting, backgrounds, and camera angles on set, creating realistic scenes without traditional green screens. By leveraging AI-powered rendering and real-time adjustments, *The Mandalorian* set a new industry standard, making virtual production faster, more flexible, and more immersive.

This isn't just related to business and Hollywood. Even the art world is being changed, where the very definition of creativity is being reconsidered. Ai-Da is an AI humanoid artist who created *AI God: Portrait of Alan Turing* using a combination of cameras, algorithms, and robotic arms. Alan Turing was a British mathematician, logician, and cryptographer whose work in breaking the Nazi Enigma code during World War II and pioneering theoretical computer science laid the foundation for modern computing and AI. To make the painting, the robot first analyzed images of Alan Turing using its camera eyes, then generated preliminary sketches through its AI-driven software. Ai-Da painted 15 different sections of Turing's face, each uniquely interpreted by the algorithm, before selecting three final pieces along with an image of Turing's Bombe Machine (Turing's invention to break the Nazi's encrypted messages).

The completed art piece went up for auction at Sotheby's with an initial estimate of $120,000 to $180,000. However, after 27 bids, it shattered expectations, selling for a record-breaking $1.08 million. This staggering price made it the most expensive artwork ever auctioned by a humanoid robot, further solidifying AI's growing role in the art world.

These are just a few of many examples that show how AI is not just hype but is making an impact in diverse areas of computer programming, business, movie making, and art. AI and GenAI are already being used by a wide range of people to do real tasks.

Moving on from hype, consider the vast scale of GenAI usage and development. Recently, OpenAI, the parent company of ChatGPT, announced that 800 million people now use ChatGPT each week. In terms of investments, the generative AI sector has attracted substantial funding from both governments and private enterprises. In 2024, global venture capital funding for AI-related companies exceeded $100 billion, marking an 80% increase from $55.6 billion in 2023. Notably, generative AI alone accounted for approximately $45 billion of this investment in 2024, nearly doubling from $24 billion in 2023.

Governments worldwide are making significant commitments to AI development. In January 2025, U.S. President Donald Trump announced a private-sector investment of up to $500 billion in AI infrastructure through a joint venture named Stargate, involving OpenAI, SoftBank, and Oracle. Similarly, the European Union launched the InvestAI initiative, mobilizing approximately $206 billion (USD) to enhance AI capabilities across member countries.

This scale of investment is supercharging the advancement of AI abilities. The rapid advancement of AI is evident in its ability to solve complex tasks with ever-increasing precision. In 2021, AI systems solved only 6.9% of the problems in the MATH dataset. The MATH dataset has 12,500 challenging math problems used in elite high school competitions. By 2023, a GPT-4-based model achieved an 84.3% success rate—approaching the 90% human baseline—and by 2025, state-of-the-art models have pushed these numbers even closer to perfection.

The abilities of AI models are advancing so well that scientists are having to design increasingly more difficult tests for benchmarking. One of the most recently designed tests is forebodingly called "Humanities Last Exam." Here's how it is described, "Humanity's Last Exam (HLE) is a global collaborative effort, with questions from nearly 1,000 subject expert contributors affiliated with over 500 institutions across 50 countries—comprised mostly of professors, researchers, and graduate degree holders." Here is an example of the difficulty of a few questions:

Hummingbirds within Apodiformes uniquely have a bilaterally paired oval bone, a sesamoid embedded in the caudolateral portion of the expanded, cruciate aponeurosis of insertion of m. depressor caudae. How many paired tendons are supported by this sesamoid bone? Answer with a number.

Or

I am providing the standardized Biblical Hebrew source text from the Biblia Hebraica Stuttgartensia (Psalms 104:7). Your task is to distinguish between closed and open syllables. Please identify and list all closed syllables (ending in a consonant sound) based on the latest research on the Tiberian pronunciation tradition of Biblical Hebrew by scholars such as Geoffrey Khan, Aaron D. Hornkohl, Kim Phillips, and Benjamin Suchard. Medieval sources, such as the Karaite transcription manuscripts, have enabled modern researchers to better understand specific aspects of Biblical Hebrew pronunciation in the Tiberian tradition, including the qualities and functions of the shewa and which letters were pronounced as consonants at the ends of syllables.

מִן־גַּעֲרָתְךָ יְנוּסוּן מִן־קוֹל רַעַמְךָ יֵחָפֵזוּן (Psalms 104:7)?

Or some questions even provide images with the questions, such as:

Here is a representation of a Roman inscription
originally found on a tombstone. Provide a
translation for the Palmyrene script.
A transliteration of the text is provided:
RGYNᵓ BT ḤRY BR ᶜTᵓ ḤBL

What's amazing about this test is both the difficulty of solving each problem and the breadth of knowledge covered. As I looked over some of the questions, I was not surprised that I couldn't answer a single question. I was a little surprised that I didn't even know what most questions were asking! At this time, most of GenAI's models, such as ChatGPT-4o, Grok-2, and Claude 3.5 Sonnet, could only answer less than 5% of the questions correctly. However, AI researchers discovered reasoning models that allow the GenAI model to think before responding, and they have more than tripled the ability to respond to nearly 15% of the questions correctly. How long will it be before the GenAI scores nearly perfect on Humanity's Last Exam?

Everything I just described underscores how rapidly and profoundly AI is reshaping our world. It's easy to be amazed—or overwhelmed—by these advancements. But beyond marveling at AI's capabilities, our most critical task is to look inward.

> The real transformation needed in the AI world isn't just in technology; it's in how we, as humans, adapt and evolve alongside it. This is precisely why our mindset matters so much.

Throughout this book, we'll explore specific mindsets that need updating and practical strategies for embracing them. By adopting a growth mindset—open, adaptable, curious—we can position ourselves not merely to survive but to be successful in this new era. Rather than viewing AI as a threat or a novelty, we must see it as an invitation to grow, learn, and reinvent ourselves.

As you turn these pages, think about your own mindset. Where might your beliefs and attitudes be holding you back from fully engaging with AI's potential? How can you actively shift toward a mindset that welcomes innovation, experimentation, and continual learning?

The journey ahead promises challenges but also extraordinary opportunities. This book will help you start that journey by helping you identify key mindsets needed to succeed in the AI-infused future.

Chapter 1

Behind the Curtain:
How AI Works

A I is an umbrella term that covers many different subtopics. Indeed, experts can't even agree on how to define it. At a basic level, AI is the ability to get computers to act like humans. You can think of AI's human-like behavior as existing on a very wide spectrum. On the left of this spectrum, consider very simple, rule-based tasks. A computer can add two numbers together like a human. On the far right of the spectrum, a computer could perform tasks similar to a human, such as carrying on an interesting conversation while cooking an omelet. The following image will help us discuss this spectrum.

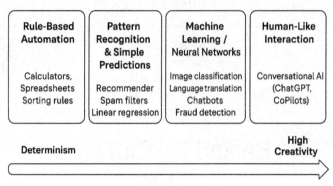

Figure 1: The AI Capability Spectrum—from rule-based tasks to human-like interaction.

Across this spectrum, computers use a diverse range of techniques to perform human-like tasks. In our example on the far left, a computer uses a calculator program to perform mathematical calculations. When a computer runs a calculator program, it carries out basic operations like addition, subtraction, multiplication, and division. These operations are straightforward and rely on predefined rules and algorithms, making them highly deterministic. The computer doesn't "understand" the math as a human does—it simply executes instructions to process numbers as per its programming.

As we move to the right of the spectrum, computers take on increasingly complex tasks that go beyond basic rule-based operations like those of a calculator. At this stage they utilize more advanced tools and techniques to analyze data, make predictions, and even "learn" from experience. For instance, they might use regression algorithms to identify patterns in data, machine learning techniques to adapt and improve over time, or neural networks to process complex information like images or language. These methods enable computers to perform tasks that require reasoning, decision-making, and adaptability, gradually resembling more human-like behavior.

Part of the challenge of defining AI is deciding if all these different tasks are considered AI or if only some on the spectrum count as "intelligence." I'm going to side-step that discussion entirely. For the purposes of this book, it is enough to know that computers are increasingly more capable of performing complex tasks on the right side of the spectrum. One of those techniques that computers use and that the media highly discusses is generative AI, or GenAI for short.

Most people have probably heard about GenAI through chatbots like OpenAI's ChatGPT, Google's Gemini, Microsoft's CoPilot, Anthropic's Claude, X's Grok, or other similar products. If you haven't heard about these apps, look one of them up and try it before continuing with this book. The book will make a lot more sense if you have some experience using a chatbot.

At the most basic level, you open one of these chatbots and have a textbox where you can type something. What you type into the chatbot is called a prompt. The textbox in a chatbot looks like a Google or Bing search box. When you type in your prompt, the computer uses GenAI to return a response. What is impressive about this technology is the ability of the computer to respond in amazing ways. For instance, I can type in a simple prompt of

```
Why did the chicken cross the road?
```

The GenAI chatbot might return:

```
To get to the other side!  🐔 🚶 Classic humour, but
if you're looking for a more creative twist, let
me know!  😊
```

When I made this simple prompt, the chatbot even returned emojis. While that is cute, what is impressive is the sophistication of responses with better prompts. I can continue my conversation with the GenAI chatbot and update my prompt to something like,

```
That is a great response, but give the same response
with a Newtonian physics twist, using as many words
as possible starting with the letter T, and add a
little bit of sci-fi humour.
```

The chatbot then returns, again with appropriate emojis:

```
The chicken traversed the thoroughfare to terminate
its trajectory towards the terrestrial target,
propelled by thrust and tethered by the tenets of
Newtonian motion. Meanwhile, a time-traveling
turkey took notes, trembling at the theoretical
turmoil this poultry pioneer could trigger in a
tachyon-fuelled timeline.  🐔 ✨ 🚀
```

Or I could ask the chatbot to "Turn that joke into a Shakespearean haiku." And it will respond with something like:

```
Why doth yon fowl tread?
'Twixt danger and promised side,
To cross fate's cruel thread.
```

You can continue prompting the chatbot in millions of different ways. Basically, if you can type it, the Chatbot can respond. A Chatbot is one example of GenAI that is designed to produce text responses.

Now, if this is all chatbots did, we would have tremendous fun, but we wouldn't accomplish much. However, you can use the simple chatbot to do far more than write simple and funny poems, songs, or bad jokes. I will share examples throughout the book, but first, I want to explain the basics of how GenAI works to help guide the mindset shifts we need to make. I will keep the explanation relatively simple, but hit the most relevant points for our discussion.

GenAI can be referred to as a model, which is to say it is a computer program that uses advanced algorithms and large-scale datasets to generate human-like text, images, audio, and other forms of content.

For our discussion, we will begin by focusing on GenAI models that only relate to text, which are called Large Language Models, or LLMs. LLMs are designed to process input data, identify patterns, and produce contextually relevant and coherent outputs that mimic human creativity and reasoning.

To build an LLM, you start by collecting a large set of data. The more data you gather, the better. To build an LLM, you gather as much text data as possible. Companies training the best models have gathered text that has been digitized, including large amounts of the Internet, digitized books, recordings transcribed into text, etc.

With this very large text dataset, the computer processes everything that is written by breaking it into smaller units called tokens. Tokens can represent entire words, parts of words, or even individual characters, depending on the structure of the model. The model analyzes the relationships between tokens by calculating probabilities—essentially predicting what token is likely to come next based on its context. For example, if the input contains the word "tyrannosaurus," the most probable next token might be "rex," but alternatives like "bones," "roars," or "exhibit" are also possible, depending on the surrounding text.

This process doesn't just consider individual tokens but also sequences of tokens, enabling the model to capture deeper patterns and context. These relationships are then encoded into high-dimensional mathematical structures called tensors— essentially arrays of numbers that represent the connections between billions of tokens. You can imagine this as an enormous spreadsheet, but in reality, these tensors are far more complex and support advanced mathematical operations on text. This encoding of text into numbers is what enables the model to generate coherent and contextually relevant outputs based on the patterns it has learned.

Once the model has been trained, a user inputs a prompt, and the system translates it into a numerical format that the model can process. The GenAI model uses its billions of learned parameters to solve a type of prediction problem: given the input prompt, what are the most likely next tokens (words, phrases, or sub words) to appear? Continuing our previous example, if the prompt is "The tyrannosaurus," the model might predict "rex" as the next token, but as previously stated, alternatives like "bones" or "roars" are also possible.

If the model always chose the most probable next token, it would produce deterministic outputs—meaning the same input would always result in the same response. This is how calculators work. I type in 2 + 3 and I always get 5. A deterministic approach is useful for tasks requiring precision and consistency, like generating exact answers or calculations. However, most users want GenAI models to generate creative and varied responses rather than predictable ones.

To introduce creativity, you can program the model to make probabilistic choices. Instead of always picking the top prediction, it can select from less probable but still contextually relevant tokens. This flexibility is controlled by a parameter called temperature. A low temperature results in more deterministic responses, favoring the most likely words. A higher temperature increases randomness, allowing the model to choose less likely words, which can make its answers more creative and surprising. For instance, at higher temperatures, "The tyrannosaurus" prompt might lead to an imaginative continuation like "wandered through an ancient jungle." At lower temperatures, the prompt "the tyrannosaurus" might lead to a response like, "rex is a dinosaur."

Finally, the model can be fine-tuned to improve its performance. This process involves providing feedback to adjust its internal parameters—the vast set of numbers that underpins its predictions. Imagine this as tweaking the numbers in the huge spreadsheet I described. Humans (or automated systems) evaluate the model's responses to specific prompts, marking them as "good" or "bad" based on quality or relevance. The model then adjusts its parameters to increase the likelihood of producing desirable responses in the future. Fine-tuning can range from minor tweaks for specific tasks to extensive retraining, depending on the resources and goals of the project.

Let's summarize this explanation into a few steps:

1. Collect a large set of text data—gather as much digitized text as possible, such as Internet content, books, and transcripts.

2. Process the text into numerical tokens—break down the text into smaller units (tokens) and represent them as numbers for computational analysis.

3. Train the model—use advanced algorithms to identify patterns and relationships among tokens, encoding these into high-dimensional mathematical structures called tensors.

4. Set parameters for creativity (e.g., temperature)—define how deterministic or creative the model should be in generating responses.

5. Fine-tune the model—adjust the model's internal parameters based on feedback to improve its performance for specific tasks. (the order of Step 4 and 5 is interchangeable)

6. Deploy the model—make it available for users to input prompts and receive generated outputs.

As you consider these six steps, it's important to understand that many people misuse the terminology surrounding LLMs. The most common confusion arises from mixing up training a model, fine-tuning a model, and prompting a model.

Training a model refers to steps 1 through 3. This process— gathering data, processing it, and learning token relationships—is typically done only by large companies like OpenAI, Google, or Meta. It requires vast resources, time, and computing power.

Fine-tuning, related to step 5, involves updating the model's internal parameters using new examples or preferences. This also demands substantial resources and is rarely necessary for everyday users.

Most people, however, interact with models through prompting— giving clear instructions, refining prompts, and iterating until the output improves. Prompting does not change the model itself, but it can dramatically affect the quality of results.

As you engage with AI tools, using these terms correctly—training, fine-tuning, and prompting—will help you communicate more effectively and avoid confusion.

This summary is a basic view into how large language models are built and function. You can build other types of models using similar techniques for images, videos, music, computer programming languages, etc. A model that processes multiple types of content, such as text, images, or audio, is called a multimodal model. There are also many other AI techniques that can build models in different ways. For this book, I will stick to a basic explanation of GenAI model building. Now I will consider how it reshapes the mindsets we need to be successful in an AI world. Many of the subsequent discussions apply to these other AI techniques as well.

CHAPTER 2

AI is Not a Calculator: Learning to Work with Uncertainty

A major update to your mindset for using GenAI centers around GenAI being probabilistic and not deterministic. As explained in the previous chapter, GenAI has a temperature parameter that allows it to be more or less creative. When the temperature parameter is set to higher values, the responses select words that are less probable, and thus, the responses can be more creative.

We already have mindsets for thinking in probabilistic and deterministic ways. When we check the weather for the chance of rain, we know to think probabilistically. That is, if we look at our weather app and it tells us there is an 80% chance of rain, we will likely take a coat or an umbrella when we leave home. When we get home and it hasn't rained, we recognize that even though there was a chance it would rain, it wasn't a guarantee it would rain.

Similarly, we are also accustomed to thinking deterministically in certain situations. When we bake a new recipe, we expect the outcome to be very close to the recipe. If we used a chocolate chip cookie recipe and the output was banana bread, we would be very shocked!

I recognize that many processes are somewhere between deterministic and probabilistic. There is a chance when we follow a recipe, it doesn't turn out quite right. Our mindset understands this for cooking, and we can adjust appropriately, even if something is not purely probabilistic or deterministic.

When dealing with computers, most of us are used to deterministic behavior. When we type numbers into Excel and add them up, we expect to get the same answer every single time. When we click on the camera app on our cell phone, it should always open the camera app. Most of our interactions with a computer are deterministic. GenAI doesn't follow this pattern and thus, we need to change our mindset. Here's a very brief example.

I input the following prompt into ChatGPT three times (using a different chat window each time): "Tell me a funny dad joke." Here are the three answers it returned.

```
Why did the scarecrow win an award? Because he was
outstanding in his field!
Why don't skeletons fight each other? Because they
don't have the guts!
Why don't skeletons fight each other? Because they
don't have the guts!
```

I hope you don't groan at those jokes as much as my kids groan at mine! More important than the quality of the humor, notice that the first response differed from the other two. The exact same prompt gave different answers. Interestingly, the second and third responses were identical—this was genuinely the case and not manipulated. When dealing with GenAI, the answers can be identical or different, and there is no way to tell what will happen before you prompt the GenAI model.

The fact that GenAI is probabilistic is critical to updating your mindset of how to use it. There are some tremendous positives and some equally tremendous downsides to this feature.

The probabilistic nature of GenAI enables creativity and variety, making it a powerful tool for tasks requiring innovation. For instance, when brainstorming marketing slogans, a user might input a prompt like "Suggest a slogan for an outdoor hiking company that is playful and funny" and receive a response like, "Take a Hike—We'll Show You the Fun Way!" Even better than a one-off response, you can ask the GenAI to give you 5, 10, or more responses. Then you can have a list like the following:

1. "Nature's Calling—Don't Ghost It!"
2. "Lost? Perfect, You're Doing It Right!"
3. "Hike More, Worry Less (About Wi-Fi)"
4. "Blazing Trails, Not Just Snacks!"
5. "Adventure Awaits—Bring Snacks!"

This gives you a list of possibilities that you can now work with. You may choose one of these directly, though in my experience that's relatively unlikely. More likely, you will find yourself generating a list of possibilities and then using the responses to help you think differently. You can then iterate until you get to an outcome that feels right. In the above example, you may really like the second option, so you can then ask the LLM to generate more responses similar to that option, or similar to that one but that evoke a different emotion. Probabilistic responses allow you to brainstorm and be creative very quickly. You never have to start with a blank page, as you can very easily get some ideas to move in your desired direction.

Probabilistic responses also enable the user of the AI tool to tailor its output based on user preferences or contextual cues. You can ask for responses to be tailored directly to the audience you care about. I find this adaptability to be very helpful in teaching. When I teach a concept in the classroom, I can ask for examples to be tailored to the interests of the students. For instance, I can change a math story problem to focus on a topic, like ballet, that I know little about, but a particular student might find it more engaging. While it was possible in the past to adapt, it is now far easier as I don't have to know anything about a topic like ballet to adjust a problem. All I must do is ask the GenAI tool to make the changes and it does the work for me.

The final benefit of probabilistic responses I'll will mention is engagement. Most people don't pick up a calculator and type things in for hours on end. The answer is always going to be the same. While useful for math, it's boring for doing anything else. In contrast, my family and I sat around generating all sorts of images using GenAI tools that combine different animals. You may have seen images generated by AI that creatively merge creatures, like an ant and an owl, into one surreal creature (see the image below). Be careful if you try it, you may spend hours generating new types of animals. The different results that we generate make it fun to use.

Figure 2: Creatively using AI to combine an Ant and an Owl.

These three benefits point to a necessary mindset shift—one that sees AI not as a replacement for human creativity but as a co-creator that enhances it. AI enables both adaptability and creativity while remaining highly accessible and easy to use. This stands in stark contrast to the portrayal of AI in science fiction and sensationalized media narratives, where it is often depicted as a force that will take control or render humans obsolete. That kind of fear-based thinking isn't productive in the real world. Instead, think of AI as a creative partner. AI doesn't replace your ideas but helps refine, expand, and enhance them.

> *Rather than simply copying AI's output or relying entirely on your own thoughts, the most effective approach is an ongoing, iterative exchange—one where human intuition and AI's capabilities combine to create something greater than either could alone.*

Currently, AI is not used to completely take human jobs away. It is just not good enough to do that in most situations. In contrast, it is taking away tasks of some jobs and allowing individuals to do things they couldn't previously do. Let me give you an example from my classroom.

For four lectures, I taught my students the basics of GenAI. We covered introductory topics of what it is and how it works. We then covered numerous examples of how it is being used in business. I also introduced some complex topics of agents, multi-agent workflows, and using AI through an API. After just four classroom sessions and the associated homework, I assigned the students to build something that would be valuable to an accountant or in an education setting. I then set them free to innovate on their own.

Before I discuss what happened, pause for a moment to think about how this assignment is different from a typical university assignment, especially an accounting assignment. Many accounting assignments are rooted in deterministic thinking. You teach students tax rules, and they correctly fill out a tax form. You explain a business scenario and the student generates a journal entry. While there is certainly judgment in many audit, tax, and financial reporting situations, the goal is very often to come to a defensible, objective, defined answer. The students are used to this. We tell them what to do, and they go do it.

In contrast, my assignment was designed to prepare students for a probabilistic world. That is, they had to generate a problem, define a solution, and then build it. The entire problem is open-ended and there is not a deterministic outcome. You can't just select "C" on the assignment like you would on a multiple-choice exam. Faced with this difference, made students felt uncomfortable as they were stuck in a deterministic mindset of doing what they were told and needed to adjust to a mindset that allowed creativity and innovation.

So, what happened? The 320+ students came to class and presented some amazing projects. I was impressed with the breadth of problems they tackled and the solutions they generated. I had students with no programming experience build functioning apps and websites. After the initial discomfort of having to break out of their deterministic thinking educational mold, they were able to use GenAI to cocreate in amazing ways.

After the presentations, I asked the students to debrief and there was near unanimity that although the project was different and hard at first, they learned more and enjoyed this project more than the typical accounting assignments given in the past. They learned that GenAI could be a cocreator and embraced the positives of the probabilistic production enabled by GenAI.

Probabilistic responses do have downsides. I teach accounting. There's an oft-told joke: 'What happened to the creative accountant? He went to jail.' As humorous as it sounds, there's truth in it. I'm really hoping my previous assignment didn't send my students on the path to a life of crime. Still, in many accounting settings, you don't want creativity. Filling out tax forms creatively will get you an interview with a cranky IRS agent! You need the tax form to be correct, every time. There are many situations outside of accounting that also require replicability to be of value. Knowing that GenAI can be probabilistic requires that the user thinks more carefully before using the tool. The user must decide if they want a probabilistic or deterministic answer.

Related to getting a different answer each time you ask a question, a more fundamental concern is that GenAI tools can hallucinate. The term hallucinate means that the response given by an AI is factually incorrect. One early example of this was asking a GenAI tool how many "r's" are in the word strawberry. It would confidently respond "2." This is a hallucination because strawberry actually has three "r's".

Why do GenAI tools hallucinate? Think back to the chapter on how GenAI works. When answering the strawberry question, the GenAI tool trained on textual data is not doing a calculation. That is, we could design a program to parse the words into individual letters and then count how many times r appears. This is not what GenAI does natively. Instead, it is looking at patterns in tokens (e.g., words and phrases) to predict the next word. It did not do math. So, it can get these predictions wrong because of its training data or simply because it wasn't designed to do that type of task.

Hallucinations can be far more problematic than the simple counting problem. An early example of a problematic hallucination was a lawyer who used GenAI to help in his legal work. His client was suing an airline in what is described as a routine personal injury suit. The lawyer used ChatGPT to help develop the case, and ChatGPT created six other cases, establishing precedents for the lawsuit. The problem? Those six cases sounded realistic but were completely fabricated. The lawyer admitted to using ChatGPT, but, apparently, wasn't aware that it is probabilistic in developing replies and doesn't work like Google in looking up legal cases that actually happened. Ultimately, the lawyer and his law firm were fined $5,000 for submitting fake citations in a court filing, and they received a lot of negative publicity around the world (I avoided using his name as he has suffered enough from being an early tech adopter who made a mistake).

There is one more lesson to teach from the experience of the lawyer. It is reported that the lawyer had apparently prompted ChatGPT to ask if it was fabricating the cases. When ChatGPT reported it was not, he trusted that answer. For hallucinations, it is not enough to ask ChatGPT if it is telling the truth or to prompt it to not hallucinate. It is a probabilistic algorithm that doesn't understand in the sense that we understand. The output may or may not be real and therefore, the algorithm cannot stop hallucinating because you simply tell it not to do so. That would be like asking it to get the math problem right, but it can't because it does not have access to a calculator. Awareness of the potential for hallucinations should significantly update your mindset on how and when to work with GenAI tools.

> *Many people have given advice that you should treat GenAI as a brilliant intern. It has access to tremendous amounts of information, but it may not perform exactly how you want it to perform. Like many interns, it is often eager to please you and will try to give you an answer even if it makes it up.*

To reduce hallucinations, consider the following suggestions.

Using GenAI as a brainstorming tool rather than expecting a single definitive answer (unless you use the tool functions that return answers and citations to those answers). By exploring a range of possibilities the AI provides, you can apply your judgment to determine which suggestion works best. This approach leverages the AI's creativity while maintaining control over the final decision. This turns the probabilistic nature of GenAI from a negative into a positive. For a tax student, this looks like having the tool return several possible treatments for a situation rather than just asking it to answer the question. The student can then research these possibilities and determine which is right.

As another example, instead of relying on GenAI to generate a complete first draft of memo, you can create the initial draft yourself or even just outline key points you want included. Then, use the AI to refine, edit, restructure, or expand on your ideas. This collaborative method ensures the output aligns more closely with your intent while reducing the risk of inaccuracies.

When crafting prompts, it's helpful to give the AI an "out." For instance, if you ask the AI to create a recipe from a list of ingredients, include a clause such as, "If you cannot combine these in an appropriate way, respond that you can't create a recipe out of these ingredients." This allows the AI to acknowledge its limitations rather than generate an illogical response because it is trying to fulfill your request.

After generating an output, you can take additional steps to verify its accuracy. Open a new conversation, input the AI's earlier response, and then ask it to evaluate the content. For example, you might prompt it to check the logic of an essay, identify potential factual inaccuracies, or highlight areas for improvement. Framing your request in this manner often yields more reliable insights than directly asking if the AI hallucinated. This can work even better if you use different models, as each model has different strengths and weaknesses.

If the GenAI tool you're using supports web searching, you can request citations for the generated content. There are also more sophisticated methods, such as building RAG (retrieval-augmented generation) models or multi-agent models with fact checkers that can help reduce hallucinations. Whatever you choose, make sure to manually verify the output and the cited sources, as GenAI models can sometimes hallucinate realistic-sounding sources, as we saw with the lawyer example.

By adopting these strategies, you can minimize the impact of hallucinations and maximize the utility of GenAI in your tasks. Do keep in mind, to date, none of these methods have been able to fully eliminate hallucinations. Even with the current state-of-the-art AI, you must be cautious with what it produces.

One particularly concerning problem with hallucinations is that they appear so correct, even when they are wrong. GenAI typically writes with flawless grammar and is quite polished. When most of us see something polished, we assume it is correct. Thus, we must fight against that mindset and be especially critical of what comes out of a GenAI tool. This will require updating our mindset to be critical of polished outputs, even more than when humans produced writing without GenAI.

We also must update our mindset to take greater responsibility for what we produce using GenAI. It is so easy to produce materials that we must discipline ourselves to do the very detailed, and often boring work of reviewing outputs. I learned this lesson when I tried using GenAI to develop test questions for my students.

To try and save some time, I asked ChatGPT to take a previous exam and generate similar questions in terms of difficulty and concepts tested that were worded differently. Faculty often update questions in this manner because exam questions can be posted online, and students can easily search for a question that is worded exactly the same way to find the correct answer. ChatGPT complied with my request and produced the questions I asked. I was cautious at first and carefully reviewed the first few questions. They were flawless. They changed the wording but retained the difficulty and the principles I was trying to test. After reviewing a couple of problems, I became lazy and didn't check the rest of the problems as carefully. Sure enough, there was a hallucination later in the problem set and the problem was mis-graded. The problem in my example isn't that I used the GenAI tool. It was that I didn't stay vigilant in reviewing and critiquing the output. You must always be careful when reviewing GenAI-generated output. This mindset is difficult to adopt because it requires constant vigilance and attention to detail. You can't take a break. Hopefully, you can learn this lesson from the lawyer's mistake and my mistake and not have to make your own mistake to have it really sink in.

We've explored why understanding the probabilistic nature of GenAI is key to leveraging its strengths. Unlike deterministic computing, which delivers predictable, repeatable outputs, GenAI thrives in creativity, adaptability, and variation. This makes it an excellent tool for brainstorming and co-creation, but it requires vigilance, critical thinking, and responsibility.

To maximize its potential, approach GenAI as a collaborative partner. Use its outputs as starting points, double-check results, and stay mindful of issues like hallucinations. Like a weather forecast, GenAI offers probabilities, not guarantees—its variability creates opportunities for innovation and fresh perspectives.

Adopting a probabilistic mindset allows you to avoid pitfalls and unlock possibilities that deterministic tools can't offer. Remember, GenAI is not a replacement for your thinking but an augmentation. Use it responsibly and thoughtfully to explore new horizons. See below how you might use a deterministic versus probabilistic mindset in several different settings.

Scenario	Deterministic Mindset	Probabilistic Mindset
Diagnosing a System Failure	Follow a step-by-step troubleshooting guide to identify a single root cause.	Use GenAI to propose multiple potential causes and prioritize them based on probabilities and context.
Setting Up a Financial Budget	Input fixed income and expense categories, expecting a rigid budget plan.	Use GenAI to explore flexible budgeting scenarios, such as "what if" analyses for variable income or unexpected costs.
Preparing for a Debate Competition	Memorize scripted arguments and pre-researched data points to counter opposing views.	Ask GenAI to simulate potential counterarguments and adaptively refine responses based on the audience or context.
Optimizing Warehouse Logistics	Use a predefined routing algorithm to maximize efficiency in item picking and packing.	Collaborate with GenAI to simulate multiple routing scenarios, balancing speed, cost, and employee workload dynamically.
Managing a Health and Wellness Program	Implement a standard wellness plan with fixed goals and activities for all participants.	Use GenAI to create personalized wellness plans based on individual preferences, goals, and past participation trends.
Responding to a Crisis Communication	Follow a standard communication protocol, issuing pre-approved statements.	Use GenAI to generate empathetic, situation-specific messaging tailored to the audience and evolving circumstances.

CHAPTER 3

It's *Not* Google

U nlike my mother-in-law, who was discussed in the introduction, most of us have adapted to the "Google world" where we regularly look up information. Researchers have found that Internet search has become so pervasive that it has fundamentally changed the way we think. The "Google effect" refers to how individuals now rely on the Internet as a source of knowledge instead of remembering information themselves. We have outsourced part of our memory to the Internet!

To adapt to the AI world, we can't use our internet searching mindset. Changing the internet searching mindset to an AI mindset will be difficult as these two mindsets conflict. Frequently, when I introduce GenAI to students or professionals for the first time, they try to fit this new tool into the old "Google mindset paradigm." They think of GenAI as a tool to look up information, which is not accurate and leads to a misunderstanding of the power of GenAI and often frustration when trying to use it.

Think back to the explanation of how GenAI works. GenAI is not "looking up" information but generating something new based on past patterns. In contrast, Google search helps you find information that already exists but does not create it.

Google retrieves, GenAI creates.

This fundamental difference between Google and GenAI requires a major shift in how we think about and use AI technology. While we've become accustomed to Google as a tool for finding information that already exists, GenAI demands a different mindset—one that sees it as a creative collaborator rather than a simple fact-retriever. However, it can also be used as a fact-retriever if used correctly. Let's look at the difference with a few examples.

Imagine you're planning a trip to Japan and want to explore unique cultural experiences. With Google, you might type "unique things to do in Japan" and receive links to blogs, travel websites, or reviews for activities like visiting a tea ceremony or exploring Kyoto's temples. If you are very good at searching, you might provide a few details of things you like to do, and you hope that Google can find a website that relates to your interests and suggests more personalized options.

With GenAI, you don't have to try and find something like what you are thinking. Instead, you can directly prompt the GenAI to, "suggest a detailed three-day itinerary for someone interested in Japan's traditional arts, including a hands-on activity each day." Instead of just linking to existing content, GenAI generates something entirely new:

> Day 1: Start your morning in Kyoto with a private lesson in calligraphy, learning the art of Japanese kanji from a local master. In the afternoon, explore a historic pottery village where you can try your hand at crafting your own tea bowl. End the day with a traditional kaiseki dinner served in a tatami-mat room overlooking a zen garden. Day 2...

See how GenAI generates a personalized plan based on your interests, offering not just ideas but actionable steps you can take. The response you receive may be entirely unique—something that's never been written before.

Now, consider a different example. You've been asked to help your child with a science project on ecosystems. With Google, you might search "ecosystem project ideas" and find lists of standard experiments, like creating a terrarium or studying water pollution. If you turned to GenAI and prompted, "What's an engaging and creative science project for a fifth grader about ecosystems?" it might generate something unexpected:

> Design a board game where each player represents a different part of an ecosystem, such as plants, herbivores, and predators. The game rules show how energy flows between species and how disruptions,

43

```
like pollution, affect the balance. Include
challenges like habitat destruction and cards that
represent positive actions like reforestation.
```

This response doesn't just suggest activities—it provides a creative and unique way to approach the topic, tailored to engage a young student. Like the first example, you could further customize your prompt to focus on ecosystem projects in your area or change it to focus on activities that are more interesting to your child.

As a final example, imagine this: you're trying to write a speech for a retirement party, celebrating a long-time colleague and friend. With Google, you'd likely search for "examples of retirement speeches" and be directed to templates or scripts to adapt. If you turned to GenAI with the prompt, "Write a humorous retirement speech for someone who loves golf and has worked in IT for 30 years," it could generate something more specific and unique:

```
We're here to celebrate [Name], who has spent three
decades solving our tech woes—and, more
importantly, perfecting their golf swing. While
they've been debugging code and building systems,
I think we all know where their real passion lies.
And now, with retirement ahead, [Name] has two
goals: to break par and to never hear the phrase
'Have you tried turning it off and on again?' ever
again…
```

GenAI crafts something original and personal instead of relying on pre-existing examples, setting the tone for your event.

These examples illustrate the fundamental difference: Google helps you find existing information, while GenAI collaborates with you to create something new. This distinction is why GenAI requires a shift in mindset—one that prioritizes creativity, exploration, and critical evaluation over simple retrieval.

This isn't to suggest that AI is better than search engines; it's just different. Each has its particular strengths and weaknesses. If you want to know who won the basketball game last night, you don't need to generate something new; you need a clear, factual answer to what actually happened. Similarly, for finding specific, verifiable information—like a recipe, historical event, or company policy—Google excels in delivering accurate, concise, and source-backed results.

On the other hand, if you're brainstorming a new way to use basketball as a metaphor in a motivational speech, GenAI is a better tool, designed to generate ideas, adapt to your context, and provide creative suggestions that wouldn't come from a list of links. This is where the real strength of GenAI lies—not in providing static answers, but in helping you explore possibilities, solve complex problems, and create something uniquely tailored to your needs. Recognizing the distinct purposes of these tools is critical to using them effectively in the right contexts.

Let's summarize the mindset shift: from finding what exists to co-creating something new with AI. To effectively use GenAI, shift your mindset from Google's retrieval-based approach to GenAI's creative capabilities. If Google is your librarian, GenAI is your creative writing partner, drawing from knowledge, but crafting something new. Unlike Google's dependence on pre-existing ideas, GenAI enables surprising possibilities and deeper personalization. While Google excels at fact-finding, GenAI thrives in creativity and problem-solving, making it important to recognize and apply these tools for their unique strengths. Updating your mindset will allow you to know when to use Google versus when to use GenAI.

I wish it was just that simple...but we have to complicate things a little bit. The creators of AI tools realized that GenAI has limitations, such as being poor at looking up facts. So, the developers decided to give GenAI some help. Many GenAI apps, like ChatGPT, now have the ability to use tools to help them overcome some of their weaknesses. For these GenAI apps, the app can examine your prompt and determine if it needs a tool to answer the prompt. If your prompt is about math, the tool might decide to use a calculator to perform the math. GenAI apps have also been given tools to search the Internet for answers. So, if the GenAI model determines your prompt needs a fact to respond, the app will design and perform a web search to find the fact and then generate the response using what it found on the web. The tools are sophisticated enough to search many websites at a time and do some basic fact-checking to ensure the websites agree. With tools, the GenAI model gives you the best of web search and generating a response because it can find the facts on the Internet and customize the response to you.

Here's a creative example of how this can be done. Assume I'm a huge fan of the Golden State Warriors basketball team and I have a favorite player on the team, Stephen Curry. I want to see who won the last game and know how my favorite player did. In this case, I could prompt the AI as follows:

"Tell me who won the last Golden State Warriors game and focus the discussion on Stephen Curry."

When I put this prompt into ChatGPT, the AI searched four different websites and then provided the following response:

```
The Golden State Warriors secured a 122-114 victory
over the Washington Wizards on Saturday night.
(Cite to website) Stephen Curry contributed
significantly, scoring 26 points before exiting the
game in the final minutes due to a left ankle
injury. (Cite to website) Head coach Steve Kerr
indicated that the injury is not serious. (Cite to
website) Curry's status for the upcoming game
against the Boston Celtics is currently listed as
questionable."
```

You can see that my response was factually accurate, because it performed web searches to get the information. Well, it was as factually accurate as the Internet is on this topic! It was relevant to what I was interested in, who won and how Curry performed. The response also provided citations to where it gathered the data (the websites included Reuters, ESPN, and others) so I can assess the accuracy of the response, if I so choose.

Contrast this with a Google search I could do to find the information. If I searched on Google, I would find a link to an article on another website, such as ESPN.com. I could then read the entire article, and it may, or may not, have information about how Stephen Curry performed in the game.

Let's summarize this chapter. Google web searches and GenAI are different tools with different purposes, although GenAI is increasing its ability to also perform web searches. The old mindset of using Google to look up information does not directly translate to a GenAI world. Instead, you need to create a new mindset to think of GenAI as a creative partner that crafts data into responses. Depending on the context, both mindsets can be useful, but don't try to force the AI mindset into the Google paradigm. This table offers a practical way to think about how your mindset might shift from the old "Google mindset" to the new "GenAI mindset."

Scenario	Old Google Mindset	New GenAI Mindset
Home renovation planning	Search for "modern living room designs" and browse image results or blog posts.	Ask GenAI to design a living room layout, suggest furniture, and create a color scheme tailored to your space and budget.
Preparing for a job interview	Look up "common job interview questions" and read advice on how to answer them.	Prompt GenAI to simulate a mock interview specific to your target role and provide feedback on your answers.
Starting a fitness journey	Search for "beginner workout plans" and read general suggestions for building fitness habits.	Ask GenAI to generate a customized weekly workout plan that fits your goals, schedule, and available equipment.

Scenario	Old Google Mindset	New GenAI Mindset
Writing a grant proposal	Search for "grant proposal templates" and piece together a document from multiple resources.	Ask GenAI to write a tailored grant proposal, emphasizing the unique strengths of your project or organization.
Resolving a customer complaint	Search for "best practices for handling customer complaints" and manually craft a response.	Prompt GenAI to draft a personalized email response to the complaint, including steps to resolve the issue.
Creating a meal plan for a family	Search for "weekly meal plans for families" and adjust recipes to suit your family's dietary needs.	Ask GenAI to create a meal plan with recipes tailored to allergies, food preferences, and time constraints.
Planning a corporate workshop	Search for "team-building activities" and compile a list of popular options.	Ask GenAI to design an engaging workshop agenda focused on your team's goals, incorporating creative activities.
Learning a language	Search for "best apps to learn Spanish" and download one based on reviews.	Ask GenAI to create a custom Spanish lesson, including vocabulary, exercises, and practical conversation scenarios.
Preparing a performance review	Search for "how to write a performance review" and follow standard templates or examples.	Ask GenAI to draft a personalized performance review for each team member, highlighting achievements and growth areas.
Traveling with kids	Search for "tips for traveling with kids" and read articles about general strategies.	Ask GenAI to plan an itinerary that balances kid-friendly activities with relaxation for adults, tailored to your destination.

Scenario	Old Google Mindset	New GenAI Mindset
Optimizing a business workflow	Search for "how to improve team productivity" and apply a generic productivity framework.	Ask GenAI to analyze your workflow details and suggest specific optimizations to save time and reduce bottlenecks.
Preparing for a difficult conversation	Search for "how to have a difficult conversation" and follow general advice from articles.	Prompt GenAI to role-play the conversation and suggest tailored approaches for your specific situation.
Decorating for a holiday event	Search for "holiday decoration ideas" and scroll through Pinterest boards or blog posts.	Ask GenAI to suggest creative holiday decorations tailored to your theme, space, and budget.

CHAPTER 4

Using GenAI is Cheating

Imagine you are sitting in a work meeting. Take a minute to visualize who is in the meeting and what the room looks like. Make this real. While sitting in this meeting, one of your colleagues starts discussing a report she recently wrote. Someone behind you proclaims to the room, "It looks like ChatGPT wrote it!" What's your reaction to the statement, and what is the reaction of everyone else in the room?

I don't know the culture of your organization. However, my guess based on almost all the meetings I have attended and conducted where something like this happens, is that the comment, "It looks like ChatGPT wrote it," is not said as a celebration of innovation and success, but rather is an indictment of the author that they did something wrong.

As an example, I was conducting introductory training at a multi-national foundation and showed the employees how to use

ChatGPT. I showed the participants how to use ChatGPT to do several tasks for their jobs very easily. There's nothing quite like showing GenAI for the first time—it feels like performing magic. "Do you want to write a performance evaluation? Upload a template, write some bullet points, click a button and…TA DAH, a finished letter!"

As the training progressed and I had the participants do some hands-on activities, I called on a woman to do a task, and she started doing it without using GenAI. I stopped her and asked why she wasn't using ChatGPT like I had been demonstrating. Her reply reflects a mindset that is pervasive when it comes to GenAI. She said, "It feels like cheating!"

This doesn't only happen in business settings. I was recently teaching a junior-level accounting course, and I asked the students to raise their hands if they had used ChatGPT the previous semester on a specific project. A few students sheepishly raised their hands. I went on to demonstrate how ChatGPT could have been used for their assignment to do it better and faster, and as I was teaching, more and more students said, "Oh yeah, I did that." After the class discussion and showing that I didn't think using AI was a bad idea, but a good idea for this assignment, I asked the students again to report how many actually used ChatGPT on the previous assignment. Almost all the hands in the room went up.

Why were the students hesitant to admit using ChatGPT for the assignment? It was not prohibited on the assignment. In fact, the faculty who had taught the previous semester had positive views of AI and encouraged using the technology.

For many employees and students, using AI is still treated like shadow IT.

Shadow IT is any technology used in an organization that is not officially sanctioned or approved. It may also not be explicitly forbidden, but it also lacks formal approval. It mostly just operates in the shadows, out of sight. Often, at organizations, it operates in a "don't ask, don't tell" middle ground. Many know technology is being used, but no one is willing to openly discuss it because of fear. The fear is often concerning that the user is doing something wrong, or fear that if someone says something, the tech will be banned, making it harder for employees to get their work done.

So, the mindset we will wrestle with in this chapter is, "Is using AI cheating?"

Let's get the easy part of this question out of the way to start. Certainly, there are situations where using AI is obviously cheating. Many teachers do not allow students to use GenAI. If they have set policies in place, and a student ignores those policies, they are cheating. It is the same in the business world. If your organization bans or puts restrictions on the use of GenAI and you use it anyway, you are being unethical. This chapter does not in any way, shape, or form argue for using AI in unethical, illegal, or immoral ways. If you are prohibited from using AI, then using it *is* cheating!

When I ask the question, is using AI cheating, I'm asking a different question than is it breaking the rules. Think back to the woman in the training I previously discussed. I was specifically hired to speak to this organization to train them on how to use AI. The organization wanted to embrace its use, yet this woman, even during a seminar specifically designed to teach its use, still felt like she was cheating. I have come across this attitude at all sorts of organizations. Many worry that, once trained, using AI feels too easy. It can seem like cheating—like you didn't work hard enough to earn the outcome. It can make work feel so easy that it feels like you are cheating.

I'm not sure where this attitude comes from. It may be rooted in the idea that effort equates to value—a deeply ingrained belief in many cultures and organizations. There's often an assumption that if something comes too easily, it must not be legitimate or "earned." This mindset stems from a long-standing emphasis on the process rather than the outcome, where hard work and long hours are celebrated as markers of worth, contribution, and quality.

This mindset makes sense in certain scenarios. I'm a hobby woodworker, with a particular interest in using the scroll saw to create intricate fretwork projects like clocks or Christmas ornaments. In this setting, spending more time is directly correlated with producing more sophisticated outputs. Even if I practice and get faster at cutting, there is a limit to my human ability such that more time spent on the task is at least a partial indicator of the quality of the output.

The same idea holds for many other situations. It is worth repeating that this book is not advocating for you to abandon all your pre-AI mindsets. Rather, it is advocating for creating new mindsets or updating your mindsets for what is now possible in many domains because of AI.

AI challenges the notion that time or effort on a task is necessarily correlated with the quality of the output. The image on the next page shows you an example of a pencil sketch made by Google's Imagen 3 GenAI model. To make this image, I started typing a prompt that describes the basics of what I wanted. I realized as I was typing the prompt, I know so little about art, I didn't even know how to describe the prompt well, "what I wanted in artistic terms." So, I took my feeble attempt at an art prompt and asked ChatGPT to improve the prompt. ChatGPT wrote my new prompt, which is listed below, and which I entered into Imagen 3:

```
Create a highly detailed and sophisticated pencil
sketch of a serene cabin nestled by a tranquil lake,
surrounded by majestic mountains. Capture the
peaceful atmosphere with refined shading, intricate
textures, and precise line work. Incorporate
advanced techniques inspired by grand master pencil
artists, such as realistic reflections on the lake,
delicate details of the cabin's wooden structure,
and the natural textures of trees, rocks, and
mountains. Emphasize depth and contrast to
highlight the serene beauty and grandeur of the
scene.
```

Here is the output:

Figure 3: Creative Image Made by AI.

For those listening to this book, realize that the image is stunning. The image created exactly what the prompt asked for. It even has an accurate reflection of the cabin and mountain in the lake, complete with the slight distortions that water makes in reflections.

This entire process took a couple of minutes. Oh, and Imagine 3 made me four different images that I could choose from.

I thought of spending a couple of hours trying to create my own version of the prompt and print that in the book. After trying for about five minutes, and not even being able to draw the cabin or mountain outline, I gave up. I'm not sure if I spent the rest of my life trying and studying, I could create an image that even approached what is seen above. I think very few people could do this, and I guarantee no artist who has ever lived on the planet could produce four versions of this high-quality image in less than two minutes.

This example seems obvious. Of course, the AI can produce an image faster that is really good! Apply this logic to the example at the beginning of this chapter. If it is so obvious that AI can make a better image, it seems just as obvious it could enhance a report. If it is so obvious that it is better, why then do we have this visceral reaction to others (or ourselves) using it that is so strong we are tempted to label them as cheaters?

While many reasons are likely to contribute to this phenomenon, I will discuss two reasons and how we should adapt our mindsets accordingly. The reasons relate to (1) tasks that are related more to process versus outcome and (2) fear and identity.

Every task is made up of a process that produces an outcome. For instance, cooking a meal involves preparing the ingredients, and the result is the finished dish. When applying for a business license, you must follow the government process of filling out forms correctly, and then the outcome is that you have a license to operate. In general, if we follow a good process, we will have a good outcome. However, there are tasks for which we care more about the process and others for which we care more about the outcome. Let me give some examples and see whether you are more worried about the process or outcome:

1. You rush your child to the emergency room, bleeding profusely from a wound to his face. Do you care more

that the emergency room surgeon stops the bleeding or that he uses the proper technique to make sure to minimize scarring from the accident? For this, you likely favor the outcome of saving your child's life over the process of how the stitching is applied.

2. You set a goal to learn a new musical instrument, like the cello. Do you focus more on perfecting your technique or on being able to play a specific song? Most musicians will focus on the process of learning how to play rather than the outcome of being able to play one song perfectly.

3. You are studying for an exam. Do you focus more on gaining a deep understanding of the material or absorbing the information for the upcoming exam? What you focus on likely depends heavily on your interest in the topic and the immediacy of the exam. From teaching students, it is most often focusing on memorizing to pass the next exam.

4. You are on a backpacking trip. Do you focus more on enjoying the journey or getting to the next campground as fast as possible? Different people will respond differently to this example. Depending on why you are on the trip could influence whether you care more about the journey (i.e., the process) or the destination (i.e., the outcome).

I reiterate that, ideally, you focus on both process and outcome because, generally, good processes lead to good outcomes. However, when answering some of those questions, you can see that there will often be a stronger focus on process versus outcomes. Let me extract some of the principles that underlie when we care more about process versus outcomes.

Principle	Process Focus	Outcome Focus
Time Sensitivity	Suits long-term endeavors where careful execution is essential.	Critical for tasks with strict deadlines or emergencies.
Purpose of the Task	Matters more when the goal is learning, skill-building, or personal growth.	Takes precedence when achieving a tangible or measurable result.
Stakeholder Expectations	Emphasized for tasks with intrinsic motivation or personal enjoyment.	Prioritized for tasks with external expectations (e.g., clients, managers, spouse).
Complexity and Uncertainty	Key for open-ended or creative tasks that drive innovation.	Main concern for clearly defined tasks.
Sustainability	Ensures sustainable results and prevents burnout or shortcuts.	May prioritize efficiency over long-term viability.
Feedback Loops	Beneficial for tasks with ongoing feedback cycles (e.g., practice, training).	Focused on single deliverable or result.
Measurement of Success	Leans toward qualitative experiences (e.g., satisfaction, creativity).	Leans toward quantitative results (e.g., revenue, test scores).

I suggest that when people are more concerned about the process, there will be greater resistance to using GenAI or other tools to accomplish or help accomplish a task. In contrast, when there is a greater focus on outcomes, people will be less likely to view using technology as cheating.

This explains how people will likely react to GenAI for different tasks. But how *should* they react? Should there be a hesitancy to using GenAI for improving processes? Should there be less hesitancy when using GenAI to achieve outcomes? To answer this question, we need to talk about fear and identity.

For most people, AI is still a new concept that is not well understood. As such, there are wildly different opinions and information about the topic. Headlines blast out conflicting narratives like, "AI could pose 'extinction-level' threat to humans and the US must intervene, State Dept.-commissioned report warns," "World Leaders Still Need to Wake Up to AI Risks, Say Leading Experts," "How we can use AI to create a better society," and "AI Aids in Early Disease Detection."

These and many more headlines can instill uncertainty or even fear in readers who are just starting to learn about this technology. If you believe AI is going to take your job, harm your children, and destroy Earth, then calling it "cheating" might be an understatement! Much of what drives the current reaction to AI is a lack of knowledge about what it is and fear of what it can do.

These reactions also bleed into identity. There is a meaningful psychological theory called social identity theory. From a social identity perspective, we find value and meaning in the groups we belong to, like cultural, professional, or personal circles. I feel very happy when my sports team wins. I'm sad when my friend has a bad day. I feel great when my company succeeds. These connections make us feel special and important by linking our personal identity to someone or something else and the successes they are having. These others shape how we see ourselves and how we relate to others.

Like fear, identity can have a strong influence on how we respond to AI. When our identity is threatened, we lash out at what threatens our identity. When our identity is strengthened, we embrace what confirms our identity. For many people, AI is threatening a very important work identity or even more fundamentally, their "human-ness" identity as being a special creature above all others. Combining being uninformed, scared, and having one's identity threatened can cause a strong reaction from others to use AI. How dare they use this "AI-thing" that can hurt us and can't possibly be better than humans!

We must fight against that mindset because it is based on several bad ideas. First, as you have learned so far in this book, AI is a tool like the computer and other tools. It can help accentuate our positives if we use it correctly. Second, AI is not inherently a threat to our identity or value as individuals; rather, it is a tool that expands our potential. Just as calculators didn't diminish the role of mathematicians but freed them to tackle more complex problems, AI helps us to focus on new challenges.

The fear and resistance to AI often stem from a misunderstanding of its purpose. While it can be about replacing human effort, it doesn't have to be. It can be about augmenting human abilities.

> *AI doesn't take away our uniqueness—it allows us to exercise our uniqueness in more ways.*

I'm not artistically talented with my hands—I can't draw, paint, or play an instrument—but AI enables me to be express the creativity in my mind. I can now create drawings, like the previous one in this chapter, with the help of AI. Similarly, for those who struggle at structured tasks, like the type of tasks accountants regularly perform, AI can enable you to perform these tasks, make fewer mistakes, and finish them much more quickly so you can get back to other tasks that you enjoy more.

Let's bring everything in this chapter full circle and tie up some loose ends. The mindset individuals have around the use of GenAI as cheating is a critical determinant of its use and ultimate success. Fear and loss of identity can contribute to an unwillingness to use AI because it is cheating and circumventing the important process of hard work leading to better outcomes. This is especially likely for tasks that typically focus more on process than outcomes.

By viewing GenAI as a tool that enhances and amplifies human abilities, you can shift your mindset about its role. With this perspective, GenAI enables you to excel at what you already do well and empowers you to accomplish things that were previously beyond your reach.

So, is using GenAI cheating? Yes, if it is expressly prohibited. If it's not prohibited, consider embracing GenAI as a powerful way to enhance—not replace—your abilities.

Let's finish this chapter with some more examples of how the new mindset will look.

Scenario	"Using GenAI Is Cheating" Mindset	"GenAI as a Tool for Enhancement" Mindset
Writing a Business Report	Believes that using GenAI undermines the writer's credibility and devalues the effort required to create original content.	Uses GenAI to draft a report quickly, focusing human effort on refining, personalizing, and adding strategic insights to elevate the final output.
Creating Visual Artwork	Feels that generating an image with GenAI is not "real art" because it doesn't involve traditional manual techniques or time-intensive skill-building.	Leverages GenAI to create visually stunning pieces, enabling the artist to focus on creative direction and innovative concepts.
Drafting a Client Proposal	Prefers to rely on manual research and formatting, considering GenAI-generated drafts as "shortcutting" or not putting in enough effort.	Uses GenAI to generate a professional draft quickly, saving time to focus on tailoring the proposal to the client's specific needs and goals.
Solving a Coding Problem	Avoids using GenAI-generated code snippets, believing it undermines the coder's skills or understanding of programming principles.	Uses GenAI to provide example code or debug errors, freeing up time to focus on improving the architecture and efficiency of the solution.
Academic Research	Considers GenAI use unethical unless explicitly approved, worrying that it circumvents the traditional hard work of reading and synthesizing academic materials.	Uses GenAI to brainstorm research questions, summarize key points, and suggest sources while ensuring proper citations and verification of data.
Preparing for a Presentation	Feels that using GenAI-generated outlines or slides is "lazy" and diminishes personal ownership of the content.	Employs GenAI to generate an outline or draft slides, enabling the presenter to spend more time on delivery and personal engagement with the audience.

Scenario	"Using GenAI Is Cheating" Mindset	"GenAI as a Tool for Enhancement" Mindset
Learning a New Skill	Views GenAI assistance as "skipping steps" and undermining the value of learning through trial and error.	Uses GenAI to accelerate the learning process by providing clear explanations, examples, and tailored practice exercises.
Writing a Speech	Considers using GenAI-generated text as inauthentic and contrary to the personal nature of speechwriting.	Uses GenAI to generate a draft, then edits it to reflect personal anecdotes, tone, and emotional resonance.
Designing a Marketing Campaign	Feels that using GenAI removes the human creativity that makes campaigns unique and impactful.	Collaborates with GenAI to generate creative ideas and variations, then selects and refines the best ones based on brand identity and audience.

CHAPTER 5

When Beginners do the Impossible

I n 1954, Roger Bannister achieved what many believed was physically impossible—he ran a mile in under four minutes. For decades, the four-minute mile had been a psychological barrier, not just a physical one. Experts and athletes alike deemed it unachievable, arguing that the human body could not endure the strain of such a feat without catastrophic consequences. The prevailing mindset of the time was that breaking this barrier was a limit not only of physiology, but also of human potential itself. Bannister shattered that mindset.

On May 6, 1954, in Oxford, England, Bannister crossed the finish line in three minutes and 59.4 seconds. His record-breaking run was not only a triumph of physical endurance and mental discipline but, perhaps most importantly, a triumph of mindset. Bannister had trained differently—not just physically but mentally. He visualized the possibility of success, disregarding the doubts of skeptics and leaning on his belief that the barrier was more psychological than physiological. His achievement was not just about speed but about challenging the deeply held belief of what was possible.

The fascinating part of this story is what happened next. Within just a year of Bannister's record-breaking run, several other athletes broke the same barrier. What had been impossible suddenly became achievable for a handful of others, despite no revolutionary advancements in training or technology during that time. The key difference was a shift in mindset. Bannister's feat redefined what humans believed they could accomplish, opening the gates for others to follow.

The mass release of AI technologies is causing a similar reconsideration of what is humanly possible in terms of work productivity. Consider, for instance, the creative challenge of composing music.

For centuries, music creation has been viewed as an intensely human and time-consuming process. Some of the most celebrated works in history took years, even decades, to complete. Ludwig van Beethoven, for example, labored over his *Symphony No. 9* for nearly ten years, crafting what many consider one of the greatest achievements in Western music. Similarly, Johann Sebastian Bach's *The Art of Fugue*, a monumental exploration of counterpoint, remained a lifelong endeavor that was left unfinished upon his death. These masterpieces stand as symbols of the immense dedication, skill, and perseverance required to create enduring art.

In contrast, iconic musical works like Handel's *Messiah*, which was composed in an astonishing 24 days, stand as testaments to human ingenuity, discipline, and skill. While this timeframe remains impressive, it pales in comparison to the rapid composition of smaller works by other artists. Mozart famously wrote the overture to *Don Giovanni* overnight, and Paul McCartney woke up with the melody to *Yesterday* essentially ready in his mind, completing it in mere hours. Nonetheless, even these instances required profound mastery of music theory, instrumentation, and creative vision—reflecting the blend of talent and effort that distinguished these musicians.

Yet today, AI has begun to challenge the boundaries of creativity and speed. Tools like Suno.AI, a generative AI platform for music, enable users to compose music in mere seconds. Unlike Handel laboring over manuscripts or even McCartney refining a melody, AI can generate complex, multi-layered musical compositions almost instantly. These tools can produce songs with full orchestration, vocal harmonies, and rhythm, all tailored to specific moods or styles simply by inputting a prompt. Furthermore, they can make things that never existed. Have you ever heard of a banjo and oboe playing a jazz duet? What about punk-rock polka fusion performed by a didgeridoo? After writing that, maybe some of these combinations don't exist for a reason!

The speed of production is also astonishing. For a $10 fee, you can make 500 songs per month, or for a $30 fee, you can make 2,000 songs per month. The potential for mass production of music has never been possible on this scale.

This radical transformation in the creative process mirrors Bannister's breaking of the four-minute mile. For centuries, creating music required intense training, talent, and extended periods of effort. With tools like Suno.AI, the process has been compressed into seconds, requiring only a conceptual idea and a prompt to produce results that would have once taken days or decades. What was once thought to require uniquely human skills and ingenuity is now accessible to anyone, regardless of musical training.

I'm not equating the work of history's greatest musicians with an AI tune made by a third grader...at least, not yet. The pace of improvement of AI is so rapid that it may be that third graders, or anyone else, can compose as well as the all-time greats in the future. Researchers estimate that AI technologies are doubling in their abilities every eight months. If that pace continues, it will not take long for anyone to be a world-class composer, writer, or artist.

The implications of this productivity boom are profound. Just as Bannister's achievement redefined what was physically possible and inspired others to surpass their limits, AI is redefining what is creatively and productively possible. The psychological barriers surrounding productivity of any type, once bound by time, skill, and effort, are being dismantled at a dizzying rate. AI is proving that the impossible—or at least the improbable—can be achieved with astonishing speed and efficiency.

Let's explore in more depth the changes we are seeing and the changes we expect to see in the near future because of AI. To do this, I'd like to discuss a metaphor by Ethan Mollick and his coauthors of a "jagged technological frontier" in their article titled, "Navigating the Jagged Technological Frontier: Field Experimental Evidence of the Effects of AI on Knowledge Worker Productivity and Quality."

The concept of the "jagged technological frontier" describes the uneven capabilities of AI when handling tasks of seemingly similar complexity. This frontier highlights that while AI performs exceptionally well on certain tasks, it struggles or even fails with others despite their apparent similarity in difficulty. In their study, the authors collaborated with the Boston Consulting Group (BCG). The researchers sought to examine how AI impacts knowledge workers across a range of realistic and complex tasks. The study involved 758 BCG consultants from around the world, representing approximately 7% of the firm's individual contributor consultants. Participants were randomly assigned to one of three conditions: no AI access, access to GPT-4, or access to GPT-4 with prompt-engineering training. By designing tasks within and outside the frontier of AI capabilities, the researchers measured performance in terms of productivity, speed, and quality of output. These measures were evaluated using a combination of human grading and AI scoring, providing a comprehensive view of AI's influence on knowledge work.

For tasks within the AI frontier—those AI could handle—results showed significant productivity and quality gains. Participants using AI for creative product innovation completed 12.2% more tasks, worked 25.1% faster, and produced responses rated over 40% higher in quality compared to those without AI. Take note of this next finding. These benefits were especially pronounced for individuals with below-average performance, whose outcomes improved by 43%, compared to a 17% improvement for above-average performers. The use of AI also leveled performance disparities among participants, suggesting its potential to democratize certain forms of knowledge work.

In contrast, when tasks fell outside the AI frontier—requiring nuanced human judgment or data interpretation—reliance on AI led to a noticeable decrease in performance. Participants using AI in these tasks were 19 percentage points less likely to provide correct solutions compared to those working without AI, underscoring the risks of uncritical dependence on AI in areas where it lacks the necessary capabilities.

This study's results show that for the right tasks, AI can have dramatic improvements on performance, but for other tasks, it can have very negative side effects. The improvements for things inside the jagged technological frontier are isolated to this study. In my research, we found that AI can perform audit risk assessments nearly four times better than unaided humans and about twice as well as humans using AI. There have been other dramatic findings from research, including a study examining the impact of AI on scientific research productivity. Researchers found that integrating AI into materials science laboratories led to a 44% increase in the discovery of new materials and a 39% rise in patent filings.[1] Similarly, in a study on generative AI, 453 professionals completed writing tasks, with those using ChatGPT showing a 40% reduction in task time, which was an 18% quality improvement.[2]

Now, not all tasks are subject to this great performance improvement. Remember the metaphor of a jagged technological frontier. GenAI technology is still so new that we are still learning where and how to apply it. Further complicating the picture is that it is progressing so fast that some things that were outside its capabilities are soon within. I learned this from my first GenAI research study.

I found out about ChatGPT 3.5 about two weeks after it was publicly released. A colleague had heard a student talking about it and mentioned it to me in the hallway. I went back to my office and tried it and was amazed that it was able to write something so coherent from a simple prompt. After trying a couple of things, I immediately wondered how well it would perform on the class material I was teaching. I opened the last exam I gave students and put in a few questions. It got the first two questions perfectly correct and then missed one. I knew I had to study this.

---

[1] https://arxiv.org/abs/2412.17866

[2] https://www.science.org/doi/10.1126/science.adh2586

To study ChatGPT, I did something different for my discipline. I put a call out on LinkedIn, emailed peers, and started a crowd-sourced research project. All faculty who would report the scores of their students on an exam and then put the questions into ChatGPT could join the research project. Over 300 faculty responded and together, we tested more than 28,000 accounting questions with ChatGPT in just two months. After analyzing the data, we found that ChatGPT 3.5 was not very good at accounting. While students scored an average of 76.7% on the exams, ChatGPT 3.5 only scored 47.5% (or 56.5% if you awarded partial credit).

The news of our study spread quickly and widely by the popular press. Headlines proliferated reporting that ChatGPT couldn't do accounting so no one needed to worry about it replacing jobs. The paper went through the review process and was accepted quickly by my discipline's standards. It was a viral hit for my accounting career.

The more fascinating part of the story is what happened about the time the paper was accepted. OpenAI released a new model, ChatGPT-4. I had numerous coauthors ask to reperform the same paper, but I declined managing that project again. Instead, three coauthors, Marc Eulerich, Aida Sanatizadeh, and Hamid Vakilzadeh, and I decided to see how well this new model would do on questions of four major accounting professional exams: the Certified Public Accountant (CPA), Certified Internal Auditor (CIA), Certified Management Accountant (CMA) and enrolled agent exams (a tax exam). Passing these exams is difficult for new accountants and is a more difficult task than passing university exams that range from introductory to graduate level.

We found that the AI models could pass all these exams using the new ChatGPT-4 model, prompt engineering techniques, and access to tools like a calculator. That is, in about three months, the AI went from not passing college-level classes to being capable of certifying in four major areas of accounting.

You should adjust your mindset to expect that AI will advance quickly.

Just because it was unable to do something you previously tested doesn't mean it can't do it shortly thereafter, given the pace of releases of new models and models with new abilities. Whatever your expectation for improvement, AI is likely going to be faster.

More than just the fast rate of improvement, is that the improvements are often not where you expect them. Much of our mindsets are built on the idea that great people can do great things. We are not surprised when super athletes perform in amazing ways. We are not shocked when the top performer at our company hits it out of the park and achieves great things. What is different with AI is that AI can distribute performance so that often the weak and poor performers see the greatest jump in performance.

You must adjust your mindset so you recognize greatness can now come from far more places.

I have another story. Not long after my GenAI research papers were published, I was approached by EY, one of the Big Four accounting firms. EY has a charitable arm called the EY Foundation, which is dedicated to advancing education through its EY Academic Resource Center (EYARC) initiative. Their website states that "the EYARC is used by more than 3,800 staff at over 900 non-profit higher education institutions across 44 countries. The Foundation has invested more than $8.9 million to support the development of these resources." The EYARC approached me about building an innovative curriculum that both uses AI and teaches about AI to help upskill students throughout the world. I put together a proposal to have the EYARC pay to hire about 12 students to work for me part-time for one year. They agreed.

I went to campus and hired accounting, information systems, and computer science students. We started meeting to discuss how we could revolutionize accounting education. It probably doesn't surprise you, but most accounting education is not high on creativity and innovation. We wanted to change that. So, we brainstormed some new ways to teach the curriculum and got to work.

The first thing we had to decide was how to deliver the new curriculum to students across the world. We researched platforms and couldn't find anything that met our needs, so we decided to build our own. So, I have 12 part-time students working for me, wanting to build an entire learning management platform and cutting-edge curriculum. Thankfully, we were crazy enough to think we could do that despite being novices. A quick note on mindsets—be willing to think big, like really, really big, as doing the impossible is now much more feasible.

We set to work. We learned how to use GenAI and embraced it in everything we did, from coding, to developing content, to making videos, to brainstorming. We were willing to try it for anything. We launched the platform less than seven months later to a worldwide audience. Despite launching just two weeks before a semester, when most faculty have settled on their curriculum, we had over 4,000 students from across the world register and use the material to complete more than 14,000 assessments during the first semester.

Within one year of release, we have posted 32 assignments. Many of these assignments do things that have never been done before in accounting education. For example, in both auditing and tax work it is very important to be able to interview others to collect evidence for auditing or to learn about their situation for filing their taxes. Many educators skip teaching these skills as it is very hard to simulate interviews in a classroom setting when there is one professor and 50 or more students. You just don't have the time or resources to teach these things. Our team built assignments that have students interview an AI-designed person and then give them specific feedback on how well they did. As another example, we built an entire virtual reality video game to give students a real-world-like experience. We had over 2,000 interns test the early versions of some of the training material, and they rated it higher than any training they'd received at school or in the firm.

What made this possible? Yes, we are fortunate to have great students at Brigham Young University. They are bright and quick learners. When you equip motivated, hard-working employees with GenAI, amazing things are possible. These are not highly experienced software engineers or expert designers of curriculum. Yet, AI made it possible for them to do things far beyond their natural capabilities in a timeline as impressive as Handel creating his music or Bannister running his mile.

In the AI world, we need to adjust our expectations of what is possible, especially what is possible by beginners or those who have traditionally underperformed. GenAI is a powerful tool that enables far more productivity for tasks inside the jagged technological frontier.

Scenario	Old Mindset	New GenAI Mindset
Breaking through psychological limits	Believe certain tasks are only achievable by experts after years of training.	Embrace the idea that GenAI can empower beginners to achieve expert-level results with minimal effort.
Rapid creative problem-solving	Rely on brainstorming sessions and groupthink over extended periods to solve creative challenges.	Use GenAI to generate multiple innovative solutions instantly, sparking ideas that might not have emerged otherwise.

Scenario	Old Mindset	New GenAI Mindset
Skill leveling in teams	Expect performance disparity between top performers and less experienced team members.	Use GenAI tools to equalize performance by providing tailored assistance to less experienced individuals, closing skill gaps.
Accelerating innovation	Assume breakthroughs require years of research, experimentation, and incremental progress.	Leverage GenAI to rapidly prototype and test ideas, accelerating innovation cycles and unlocking new possibilities.
Overcoming beginner barriers	Beginners struggle to produce high-quality work due to lack of expertise and resources.	Empower beginners to achieve expert-level outcomes using GenAI as a powerful augmentation tool.
Customized education	Deliver standardized education that improves performance gradually and often unevenly.	Use GenAI to personalize learning experiences, enabling rapid skill acquisition and equitable outcomes.
Redefining productivity expectations	View productivity gains as incremental and limited by human effort and time constraints.	Adjust expectations to account for exponential productivity improvements enabled by GenAI.

CHAPTER 6

Learning will Never
be the Same

When I was a doctoral student at Indiana University, I frequently took the bus to work. The bus would drop me off on one side of campus, and the walk to the other side of campus became a therapeutic break from my daily work. Doctoral programs are intense, so the time outside getting some light exercise was a great blessing.

One of the challenges of my doctoral program was the tremendous amount of reading we had to do. In addition to the volume, the reading wasn't easy. Imagine reading about the intricacies of endogeneity in econometrics—grappling with instrumental variable selection, dealing with simultaneity bias, and dissecting complex identification strategies, all while navigating proofs that seem to defy intuition. In psychology, psychometrics presented its own labyrinth of latent variable modeling, requiring a deep understanding of factor loadings, structural equation modeling, and the delicate balance between validity and reliability in measurement. Meanwhile, in accounting, accrual models demanded parsing through earnings management detection techniques, distinguishing discretionary from non-discretionary accruals, and unraveling the nuanced estimation errors in Jones-type models.

If you didn't understand that last paragraph, you are not alone. I didn't understand it either! It felt like I spent as much time looking up words as reading the actual papers. So, when I was neck-deep in these dense papers, the walks to and from the bus stop served as a mental escape. One of my favorite things to imagine was superpowers that I wished I had. I remember many times wishing I had the superpower of being able to touch a paper or book and immediately know, understand, and remember everything in the paper or book. I dreamed of how nice it would be to walk around the library, touch all the books, and just know everything.

Today, GenAI makes this dream of instant understanding possible on nearly every phone and laptop. You can text, type, or even talk to an AI chatbot and it knows what everything in that previous Ph.D.-dense paragraph meant. I'll prove it. I asked ChatGPT to rephrase the Ph.D.-dense paragraph at a third-grade level of education and it produced the following:

```
Imagine having to read really hard books that use
big, confusing words. In economics, I had to learn
about how to find the real cause of something when
many things are happening at once. In psychology,
```

I had to figure out how to measure things we can't
see, like feelings or intelligence, and make sure
the numbers actually mean something. In accounting,
I had to understand how companies report their
money and figure out if they were being honest or
trying to make their numbers look better than they
really were. Every topic felt like a big puzzle,
and even after reading for hours, the answers
weren't always clear.

Think about how amazing and transformative what I just did really is. I took something incredibly complex and barely understandable to a Ph.D. student and made it accessible to virtually anyone.

GenAI is going to dramatically effect learning.

We are starting to see the power of GenAI to transform learning. To illustrate GenAI's transformative potential, let's consider the real-world educational initiative sponsored by the World Bank. The World Bank is an international financial institution that provides loans and grants to governments of low- and middle-income countries to help them develop their economies and reduce poverty. It focuses on funding projects that improve infrastructure, education, healthcare, agriculture, and economic stability.

In mid-2024, the World Bank funded a study in Africa to see how education would change if they provided GenAI to 800 senior-secondary students (high school students in their final years). The teachers acted as "orchestra conductors" to the students, guiding them through their learning for a six-week period. The study focused mainly on English language proficiency, but also on AI comprehension and digital competency.

The results of the study were amazing. Compared to a control group that did not use GenAI, the GenAI students accomplished the same learning in just six *weeks* what took the other students an estimated two *years* to learn. This approach outperformed 80% of other documented education interventions. What's even more impressive is that the teachers had to devote a significant amount of time to teaching the students how to use a computer before they could even interact with the GenAI chatbot.

There was another very interesting finding in this study. The researchers also found that the benefits were especially pronounced for female students. Female students started the study with much lower baseline performance and the usage of GenAI helped close the gap for the female students compared to their male counterparts.

Think about the superpower these African students received from using GenAI. They learned two years of content in just six weeks. Think about how much further these students could advance if they continue to use GenAI for the next two years.

As with every other area we have discussed, GenAI has the power to transform education. We will chat more about this potential in this chapter, but I want to raise a warning flag before we continue. I think GenAI also has the potential to wreak havoc with learners.

As parents and educators, we are going to have to be very careful and diligent in how we apply GenAI to education. Let's revisit my superpower example to explore why GenAI could also pose challenges to education. To see these risks, let's start by having ChatGPT define learning.

```
Learning is the process of acquiring knowledge,
skills,    attitudes,    or    behaviours    through
experience,  study,  or  teaching.  It  involves  the
ability  to  process  information,  adapt  to  new
situations,  and  improve  performance  based  on  past
experiences.  Learning  can  be  intentional  (such  as
studying  for  an  exam)  or  unintentional  (such  as
picking  up  social  norms  through  observation).
```

Let's focus on learning as a process. As I reflect on my experience as a Ph.D. student, what stands out to me is not what I learned, but what I became because of the experience. I remember a few facts from the papers and books I read, but more than the facts, I now think differently. I approach problems differently. I am a different person because of the learning experience. For example, before my Ph.D., I approached problems by looking for direct answers. But through the Ph.D. struggle, I learned to navigate uncertainty, see alternatives, and think critically about evidence and theories. The process changed me.

Contrast this with what might have happened if I had ChatGPT during my Ph.D. program, and I used it in inappropriate ways. Imagine what I could have done to get through the program. If I was assigned a 50-page paper, I could have summarized it into four paragraphs that I understood. I could have asked the GenAI tool to find two to three weaknesses in the paper I could bring up in discussions. I might have asked GenAI to write an extension paper and then tweak it to make it my own. With GenAI, I could have had all the right answers, but at what cost? Would I have become something better if I had used GenAI instead of the stretching, difficult process I went through?

The process of true learning is to help us become something more than just human computers that can regurgitate facts. I think we lose sight of this in much of our current learning that is governed by tricky quizzes, end-of-semester exams, professional licensure exams, or completing dull professional training. We focus so much on the outcome of learning that we forget about the process of learning. This is the first mindset shift we need to have to be successful learners in an AI world.

Learning is not only, or even mostly,
about the outcome of the learning.
It is about the process.

This is more easily seen in learning that is not cognitive in nature. Let's look at a pianist and their learning. When a pianist learns to play a complex musical piece, the real learning isn't just about hitting the right notes in the right order. That is akin to memorizing facts. It's necessary but not sufficient to be a musician. For the pianist, it's more about the process—hours of practice, the slow and sometimes frustrating repetition that builds muscle memory, the careful listening that sharpens ear training, and the deep emotional connection that transforms mechanical playing into true artistry. If a pianist focused only on playing a piece perfectly for a test, they might master the technical execution but never develop true musicality. It is the process—the struggle, the refinement, the gradual internalization of the music—that turns a pianist into an artist.

Now, you can push back and say no one wants to listen to the pianist who plays wrong notes. The pianist has to worry about the outcome. I agree, but focusing on the outcome will not produce the same result as focusing on the process. By focusing on the outcome, the pianist might eventually be able to play the song correctly. Still, they will not become a musician—someone capable of applying what they have learned to all music. In contrast, the pianist who focuses on learning to play music will eventually be able to play the song correctly and transfer everything they learned to other songs.

An exclusive focus on outcome—like playing a piece perfectly—may lead to technical proficiency, but it won't create a musician. Likewise, memorizing facts might yield short-term success in academic learning, but without deep engagement in the process, the learner is much less likely to develop transferable skills. This same principle applies to learning in an AI-driven world. If we allow AI to simply give us answers, we might succeed on assignments and tasks, but we risk missing out on the deeper transformation that comes from wrestling with ideas, making mistakes, and ultimately growing as thinkers.

So, what can focusing on the process of learning in an AI world look like? To give you an example, I first briefly introduce a revised version of Bloom's taxonomy. Originally developed by the educational psychologist Dr. Benjamin Bloom in 1956, Bloom's Taxonomy is a hierarchical classification of cognitive skills used in learning. It organizes educational objectives into levels of increasing complexity, beginning with basic recall of facts and progressing toward higher-order thinking skills, such as analysis, evaluation, and creation. The framework has been widely used to design curricula, assessments, and instructional strategies across various disciplines.

In 2001, educational researcher Dr. Lorin Anderson and educational psychologist Dr. David Krathwohl revised Bloom's Taxonomy to better reflect modern learning and cognitive processes. The key updates included changing the category names from nouns to action verbs and emphasizing learning as an active process. The revised taxonomy consists of six stages: Remember, Understand, Apply, Analyze, Evaluate, and Create, each representing a progressively deeper level of cognitive engagement.

To illustrate how this revised taxonomy applies to real-world learning, consider the case of a medical student progressing through the six cognitive steps in the Bloom's taxonomy. At the Remember stage, the student memorizes anatomical terms, building the foundational knowledge needed for more advanced concepts. Moving to the Understand stage, they begin to explain how blood circulates through the heart, demonstrating comprehension beyond simple recall. As they advance to Apply, they use their knowledge in a practical setting by performing a basic physical examination on a patient. At the Analyze stage, the student starts to break down complex patient symptoms, distinguishing between different possible diagnoses based on medical principles. In the Evaluate stage, they critically assess various treatment options, determining the most effective approach for a given patient and justifying their decision based on clinical evidence. Finally, at the Create level, the student synthesizes all their knowledge and experience to design a new method for improving patient treatment, contributing to innovation in the medical field.

Now, I produce a table of what learning might look like in this scenario when GenAI is used appropriately to enable the process of learning versus if it is used to circumvent and short-circuit the process of learning.

Cognitive Step	Traditional Method (Without GenAI)	Correct Use of GenAI	Incorrect Use of GenAI
Remember	Memorizing anatomical terms using flashcards or textbooks.	Using AI-generated quizzes and spaced repetition systems to reinforce memory.	Relying on AI-generated summaries without actively engaging in recall practice.
Understand	Explaining blood flow using diagrams and classroom discussions.	Interacting with an AI tutor that explains complex processes dynamically with adaptive feedback.	Copying AI explanations without verifying accuracy or deepening understanding.

Cognitive Step	Traditional Method (Without GenAI)	Correct Use of GenAI	Incorrect Use of GenAI
Apply	Performing physical exams on standardized patients or classmates.	Practicing with AI-powered virtual patients that provide instant feedback on diagnostic accuracy.	Letting AI generate full diagnoses without developing hands-on skills in real clinical settings.
Analyze	Identifying disease patterns by studying case files and medical literature.	Using AI-driven analytics to detect patterns in patient case studies and lab results.	Accepting AI conclusions without critically analyzing data and underlying assumptions.
Evaluate	Comparing treatment options through peer-reviewed research and expert consultations.	Leveraging AI tools to compare real-world treatment outcomes and support clinical decision-making.	Using AI to justify pre-existing biases rather than critically assessing medical evidence.
Create	Developing a new patient care model based on clinical observations.	Collaborating with AI to prototype new diagnostic techniques or personalized treatment plans.	Blindly accepting AI-generated research without verifying ethical, clinical, or practical validity.

Imagine the differences between the doctors who used GenAI appropriately and those who did not. The ones who use it appropriately are going to be like the African students who have progressed and know far more than current non-AI doctors. These doctors will have expanded their knowledge and abilities to be better doctors. In contrast, the doctors who use GenAI to circumvent the learning process to just focus on the outcome are not ones I would trust with my care. They didn't really learn to be a doctor. They "cheated" their way through the learning process.

I'm going to continue focusing on students, but I will turn to my accounting students to share how GenAI usage may differ significantly throughout the learning process. This, too, will require a mindset shift to realize that GenAI usage for learning will vary based on the expertise of the learners.

One of the topics I teach students is how to write computer program code, specifically SQL, to analyze data contained in databases. When students start in my class, they are beginners and know almost nothing about coding SQL. At this stage of learning, I have the students read about how to write code and practice writing code. I restrict their use of GenAI to answer the questions.

At this stage in their learning, the questions I ask the students are so simple that GenAI would get a perfect score on everything they write. It is the same as grade-school students who could use a calculator to get every math question correct, even though they do not understand addition or subtraction. At this stage of learning, I do use some GenAI. I use GenAI to evaluate their answers and explain when they are wrong, what they did wrong, and then let them try to fix it until they get it correct. That is, GenAI is a tool to help them learn rather than a crutch supporting ignorance.

Reading this example, you might ask, so, if GenAI can answer all the questions about SQL correctly, why do I have them learn it at all? To answer this, let's consider video games.

There are many video games that require the player to perform certain tasks to get to the next level. Upon getting to another level, they are granted additional powers and abilities. When designing video games, you often create the first levels to teach skills the player will need to use their new powers and abilities. For instance, in a platformer game, the first level might teach a player how to jump over obstacles, dodge enemies, or collect power-ups. At this stage, the game guides them, ensuring they develop foundational skills that they will need to use more independently as they progress. If the player were simply given all the abilities upfront without learning the basics, they might struggle to use them effectively in more complex situations.

For tasks that eventually require greater skills, it is important to help students develop the basic skills first, without additional assistance. In my class, the students need to learn some of the basics of SQL code, not because writing the code is that important, but it is important for them to understand how to structure the data in databases, how to combine it in different ways and most importantly, how it can be mistakenly used and produce incorrect output.

As my students increase their abilities and move on to other topics, I allow them to make greater use of GenAI to perform basic tasks. At this point, I often allow the students to use GenAI to brainstorm different solutions, help write basic code, or explain why code does or doesn't work. At this stage of expertise, GenAI becomes a tool to enable the students to do more, and this doesn't hurt their learning because they have acquired the basic knowledge to move forward.

Once reaching mastery or near mastery, the students can use GenAI in any way to perform increasingly complex or new things. While my students haven't achieved mastery yet, I expect that when they do, they may invent entirely new ways of doing when they combine their expertise with the AI superpower. In the hands of an expert, AI will allow them to do things that were not even considered in the past.

If you are a parent or educator thinking about AI and education for your children, create a mindset to think about when AI is best applied based on your student's expertise. As a new learner, it is helpful to use it to explain and provide additional practice. As they master basic skills, it can then transition to be more of a partner in producing output. After the student becomes an expert, the AI and the human merge in their abilities to produce outstanding results.

This discussion about when to use AI for learning is predicated on the idea that there is a progression of knowledge. This is common for most types of learning. Math progresses from basic math to algebra to calculus, etc. However, some examples of knowledge do not progress in the same way and may be fully automated by AI. In this case, learning these things should likely disappear.

For instance, data entry and basic clerical work is a domain where tasks remain relatively static—there's little complexity beyond accurately inputting information into databases. AI can now handle this process with near-perfect accuracy, making human involvement largely unnecessary. There's no longer a need to teach employees how to manually enter data from documents.

As a historical example of this shift, consider NASA in the mid-20th century. During the early days of space exploration, NASA employed teams of humans who were actually called computers. These people were highly skilled individuals, often women, who manually performed complex mathematical calculations for orbital mechanics and engineering designs. These workers were instrumental in launching the first American astronauts into space. However, as digital computers became more powerful and reliable, NASA transitioned away from human calculation teams, ultimately rendering the role obsolete.

Just as NASA's transition to digital computing reshaped the workforce, AI-driven automation is now eliminating jobs that once required human expertise. The lesson from history is clear: when a domain consists primarily of repetitive tasks that do not require a progression of knowledge, automation will eventually take over. In terms of learning, for these tasks, there is much less, or even no need to continue learning those tasks.

I'll close this chapter with one final mindset change that is needed. I will illustrate the change in mindset with a quote by Jason Pikoos, a friend of mine who is the managing partner at the Connor Group, a financial consulting firm. He stated, "In this world of super-sonic technological innovation, learning will be PART of our JOBs versus something we only do to GET the JOB."

This quote underscores an important reality in the AI era: change isn't just happening—it's accelerating. To thrive in this fast-moving landscape, the ability to learn continuously is just as important as what you learn. I created an AI-generated animated visualization to illustrate how quickly individuals can fall behind if they don't keep pace with evolving knowledge. The animation depicted several people running, symbolizing the race to stay relevant in an AI-driven world. The key insight was striking—those who start learning now may find the pace challenging, but they can stay caught up if they are diligent and consistent. However, the longer someone waits to begin, the harder it becomes to catch up. The final figure in the running visualization never starts running at all, and before long, fades into irrelevance.

The message is clear: in a world shaped by AI, standing still isn't an option.

The rapid learning gains of African students using AI, the transformative power of GenAI in simplifying complex Ph.D.-level concepts, and the historical shift from human computers at NASA to digital automation all illustrate the evolving nature of learning. These stories highlight why embracing the process over outcome mindset is crucial—true learning isn't about shortcuts but about deep intellectual transformation. They also reinforce the progressive learning mindset, where AI should be a tool that adapts to a learner's stage rather than a crutch that replaces fundamental skill-building. Just as NASA moved past human computation, some skills will inevitably become obsolete, requiring an automation and obsolescence mindset to focus learning efforts where human expertise still adds value. Finally, as Jason Pikoos warns, learning must be continuous—AI is advancing too rapidly for anyone to rely on past knowledge alone. Those who embrace this continuous learning mindset will not just keep up with AI but will harness it to drive innovation and success.

Scenario	Wrong Mindset	New GenAI Mindset
Approach to Learning	Focus on memorizing correct answers and passing exams.	Engage in deep learning, valuing the process over just the outcome.
Using AI for Learning	AI is a shortcut to avoid struggle and get quick answers.	AI is a tool for guidance and augmentation, used appropriately at each learning stage.
Skill Relevance	All skills should be taught equally, even if automation makes them obsolete.	Prioritize learning that builds expertise and critical thinking while allowing AI to handle repetitive tasks.
Progression of Learning	All learners should use AI in the same way, regardless of experience level.	AI use evolves: Beginners engage deeply, intermediates get guided help, and experts collaborate with AI for innovation.
Lifelong Learning	Learning is something you do to get a degree or a job, then stop.	Learning is continuous—staying ahead requires ongoing skill development and adaptation.
Catching Up to AI Innovations	AI is moving too fast; it's impossible to keep up.	Start learning now—those who delay will struggle to catch up, but those who embrace AI will thrive.

CHAPTER 7

Becoming an AI-Centaur:
The Future of Expertise

To begin this chapter, let me introduce John von Neumann. Born in Budapest in 1903, von Neumann was recognized early on as a mathematical prodigy with an extraordinary natural aptitude. Popular accounts from his youth tell of a child who could perform complex mental calculations and had an exceptional memory; some stories even claim that by the age of six, he could mentally divide eight-digit numbers and recite pages of text after a single reading.

His formal education led him to some of Europe's leading institutions of learning, where he made significant contributions in several mathematical fields. Yet, von Neumann was not solely a theoretician. He was equally adept at applying his skills to practical problems, a quality that set him apart from many geniuses throughout his career.

His contemporaries held him in high esteem. For example, Nobel laureate Eugene Wigner, who had known von Neumann since their early days in Budapest, recalled that even among Hungary's renowned scientific talents—the so-called "Martians"—von Neumann stood out. Likewise, various recollections suggest that both Albert Einstein and Edward Teller expressed deep admiration for his intellect.

The lore surrounding von Neumann's computational speed and problem-solving ability is almost legendary. At Princeton's Institute for Advanced Study, colleagues observed that he could listen to a complex problem and then provide a solution almost as if by intuition. One frequently told story describes how, when Hans Bethe, a noble prize winner himself, wrestled with a difficult equation for hours, von Neumann quickly offered not only a solution but even an alternative method—an anecdote that, while likely apocryphal in its exact details, has come to symbolize his remarkable capabilities.

Beyond his rapid mental computation, von Neumann made lasting contributions across multiple disciplines. His pioneering work in game theory helped lay the groundwork for modern economic analysis; his ideas on computer architecture continue to influence the design of contemporary computing systems; and his research on shock waves and fluid dynamics has impacted fields ranging from aerodynamics to nuclear technology. During World War II, his expertise proved crucial to the Manhattan Project, particularly in the mathematical modeling essential for optimizing nuclear implosions.

This brief history sets us up nicely to talk about expertise. Von Neumann will serve as my example of a pre-GenAI expert. While he is undoubtedly an outlier, even among geniuses, he demonstrates the ideal of an expert, someone with tremendous abilities built on deep theoretical knowledge, rapid problem-solving, and a unique ability to integrate insights from various fields. While von Neumann was likely born with many of these incredible talents, he refined them with years of hard work and experience.

We have the same mindset and perception of experts, whether born or created through diligent work. These are individuals of incredible ability who have the capacity to accomplish great things. Let's see how our mindset about expertise needs to change in the GenAI world by discussing another expert, Gary Kasparov.

Born in 1963, Gary Kasparov rose to prominence as one of the greatest chess grandmasters ever, revered for his incredible strategic mind, mastery of the game, and fierce competitive spirit. A combination of natural ability and unmatched dedication propelled him to the top, where he dominated the chess world. However, his reign, and the reign of all human chess players was about to end when Kasparov played IBM's Deep Blue in 1997 for the second time. Deep Blue was an IBM supercomputer designed to play chess.

Kasparov had already cemented his legacy as one of the greatest chess players of all time. He had been World Chess Champion since 1985, his reign defined by an aggressive, deeply intuitive style of play that blended deep strategic vision with extraordinary tactical precision. He had previously faced Deep Blue in 1996 and emerged victorious, defeating the machine 4-2. However, IBM's engineers took that loss as a challenge. They upgraded Deep Blue, refining its algorithms and increasing its processing power, making it a vastly stronger opponent when the rematch was set for May 1997.

The match, held in New York City, was played over six games, and from the outset, it was clear that this was not the same Deep Blue Kasparov had previously bested. The supercomputer, now capable of evaluating up to 200 million positions per second, played with a newfound depth and precision.

Kasparov won the first game, showcasing his legendary skill by exploiting Deep Blue's mechanical rigidity. However, in Game 2, something unprecedented happened. Deep Blue played a move that stunned Kasparov—move 37, Be4. To many observers, the move appeared oddly human, almost as if the machine had demonstrated a long-term strategic understanding rather than merely executing brute-force calculations. This unsettled Kasparov, who later described the move as being so unexpectedly strong that it shattered his confidence. Whether the move was the result of complex computation or simply a coincidence of the system's programming remains debated, but its psychological effect on Kasparov was undeniable.

By Game 4, Kasparov's frustration was mounting. He struggled to find weaknesses in Deep Blue's approach. The machine's immense processing power allowed it to avoid blunders and exploit small inaccuracies with ruthless efficiency. Kasparov, known for his resilience, began to falter. Then, in Game 6, the unthinkable happened—Kasparov resigned after just 19 moves, suffering an uncharacteristically swift defeat. It was a shocking conclusion to the match, one that left the chess world reeling. For the first time in history, a reigning World Chess Champion had been defeated in a match by a computer. Kasparov's loss shook the world. Many believed a computer could never beat the best humans at chess. The view that humans were always superior to computers crumbled.

What's more interesting than a computer beating the grandmaster is what happened next. After losing to Deep Blue, Kasparov had an idea to hold a chess tournament where humans and computers could cooperate as teammates. In 1998, Kasparov teamed up with a computer program to face another chess grandmaster, Veselin Topalov, who teamed up with a different computer program. Each player had the final say in what move they made, but they were allowed to consult with their computer partner. The human directing the computer was referred to as a centaur team. This type of chess has continued to evolve, where individuals, teams of individuals, and computers come together to compete against others.

The visual of a centaur is a powerful metaphor for the future of expertise in an AI world. A centaur is a mythological creature with a human upper body and the lower body of a horse. This combination was exceptionally powerful. In the modern world, experts will be AI-centaurs: combinations of humans and computers running powerful AI programs. These AI-centaurs will blend the strengths of human insight with AI's computational power to generate remarkable outcomes.

For the rest of the chapter, I will refer to von Neumann, Kasparov, and a hypothetical centaur. To make it easier, let's give this centaur the name Symbio—to represent the interplay between human(s) and AI(s). I chose this name as symbiosis is a biological term that refers to a mutually beneficial relationship between two different organisms—or in our case between human and machine. Let's start by discussing how we need to adjust our mindsets about expertise in the AI world.

To start, expertise no longer exists solely in individuals. This has been changing for some time, even illustrated by Kasparov figuring out that teams usually outperform individuals. This change is likely to accelerate, especially as AI agents are developed and deployed. Agents are autonomous AI systems capable of perceiving their environment, making decisions, and taking actions to achieve specific goals—often with minimal human intervention. Here's an example of how an agent and multiple agents might work in a hospital.

Imagine you walk into a hospital. Rather than being greeted by a receptionist, you are greeted by a virtual assistant who asks you about your symptoms and needs. As you sit down, this virtual assistant passes your information to an AI triage agent who analyzes the seriousness of your symptoms and the current workload of the medical staff, and then decides when you will see the nurse. When the nurse calls you back, various measures are taken and another AI agent assists the nurse in updating your medical file and passing the information to a diagnostic agent that will assist the doctor in taking all the information you have provided, plus all the information contained in your medical files, to help the doctor diagnose your problem.

Notice that in this problem, multiple AI programs interact. These programs are called agents—autonomous AI systems that can perceive their environment, make decisions, and take actions to achieve specific goals. Think of each agent like a digital coworker with a specialized role: one agent might focus solely on triaging symptoms, another might handle scheduling and logistics, and a third might recommend treatment plans based on your medical history. These agents don't just follow static rules—they can reason, plan, and adapt in real time. Even more impressively, agents can be designed to collaborate with one another, passing information back and forth like a well-coordinated medical team. In some experimental settings, agents are also programmed to compete, helping teams test multiple approaches and choose the best-performing one. This coordination between humans and intelligent agents forms the foundation of a new kind of expertise—Symbio, where decision-making is distributed, dynamic, and deeply personalized.

In this case, Symbio is a team of human and AI doctors, assistants, and nurses that work together to provide better care than any individual doctor. In the past, there was a team consisting of a receptionist, nurse, and doctor, but these individuals usually performed their individual tasks and then passed you on to the next person. Each had expertise in their domain, but it was not combined and did not reinforce and help what others were doing. With the healthcare Symbio, the receptionist AI might detect something in your voice that the diagnostic AI could use to help inform the doctor.

AI agents are rapidly being developed and deployed. Most technologists predict that there will be billions of AI agents that are each designed to perform their individual tasks and then combine with other agents and humans to coordinate in producing amazing things. Expertise will reside in these networks of agents and humans working together. Very few von Neumann's will make breakthroughs in the future. Instead, breakthroughs are going to come from teams. Start thinking about expertise as a collaboration of AIs and humans.

As an early example of the power of human-AI teams, consider the study conducted at Procter & Gamble involving 776 professionals, where researchers tested how Generative AI could enhance real-world product development. The results were impressive: individuals using AI performed at the same quality level as two-person teams working without AI—effectively showing that AI can replicate the benefits of collaboration. Even more impressively, teams augmented with AI produced solutions that were 39% higher in quality compared to individuals without AI and completed their tasks in 12.7% less time. These AI-enhanced teams were also three times more likely to generate top

10% solutions compared to the control group. Perhaps most fascinating, AI also reshaped expertise boundaries—participants were more likely to produce well-rounded, interdisciplinary ideas, regardless of their original background. And it didn't just affect performance: emotional benefits typically reserved for human collaboration, such as increased enthusiasm and reduced frustration, were also replicated. In short, AI didn't just help individuals do more—it made them feel more connected, capable, and creative.

To become an expert in this new era, you will need to be able to collaborate with technology and with others. This is yet another differentiator of expertise in the future. Most people think of expertise as something rooted in knowledge or raw ability—a mastery of hard facts, techniques, and strategies that set individuals apart—von Neumann could divide numbers, memorize text, or perform other feats of knowledge. Rarely do we consider qualities like collaboration, adaptability, or even interpersonal skills as central to what makes someone an expert. Expertise in the AI world will include individuals who excel at these human qualities as they will have to work with teams to get the most out of each other. It is not just those who can work with the tech that will be experts, but those who can work with the tech and others who will be the greatest experts.

Moving beyond the collaborative nature of expert teams, we must look at what Symbio will have to know. I think every parent has heard their child who is learning math, "Why do I have to learn how to do this? I can just put it in the calculator!" When I was kid, a parent or teacher would respond, "Because you won't always have a calculator in your pocket." That answer was no longer sufficient once smartphones became ubiquitous.

Most parents and teachers struggle to answer this question. Why should we learn how to do math when a tool can do it better for us? We often tell our children or students that learning how to learn is important. Sometimes we argue that someone needs to know how to program the computer, or we fall back on the classic lines like "it builds character" or "I had to learn it this way." In the end, we continue teaching math without using a calculator—but the truth is, many people could live perfectly well in today's society without ever needing to do math without a calculator.

In an AI world, the calculator expands to every other domain of knowledge. With GenAI installed on my phone, I have the knowledge that rivals the greatest thinkers that ever walked the earth. I don't just have it in math, but philosophy, physics, accounting, music, literature, medicine, architecture, law, psychology, engineering, history, linguistics, astronomy, economics, political science, culinary arts, robotics, anthropology, genetics, graphic design, theology, environmental science, cybersecurity, cinematography, fashion, meteorology, and the list goes on and on. If an AI knows everything and is "expert" in everything, what is the role of knowledge in terms of expertise?

To me, this is a transformative shift that we must make in our mindset about expertise in the AI world. Symbio knows virtually everything. Therefore, expertise is less about knowing and more about wisdom. A lay definition of wisdom is the ability to apply knowledge. My kids like the joke, "Knowledge is knowing that a tomato is a fruit, wisdom is not putting it in the fruit salad." Our new AI expert, Symbio, will know how to interpret and apply knowledge.

Let me illustrate based on a discussion I had on an airplane. I was flying home from a presentation, and I was sitting next to a man, and we casually started chatting about our work. I told him that I was an accounting professor and focused a lot of my time and attention on ChatGPT. He kind of laughed and said that AI was overhyped. I thought...challenge accepted.

I asked this man what he did, and he said he designed high-end hotel entrances. I pulled out my laptop, opened an AI image generator, and asked him to describe a fictional hotel entryway. I don't remember exactly what he described. It wasn't nearly this elaborate, but it was something like, "A grand Victorian hotel entrance featuring tall glass panels, rich walnut accents, and elegant jade highlights." I typed it into the image generator, and it created a beautiful image of a hotel entryway. The man took out his phone, texted his partner, and said he needed to subscribe to AI. His mindset was updated as he saw the power of Symbio.

I don't have knowledge of architecture, design, or hotel entryways. I am not an expert in any of these fields. However, I did have the wisdom of asking an AI that knows all these things to produce something. That is one example of the future of expertise—being able to apply knowledge through asking AI agents to answer our questions.

So, do we need to know anything if our AI agents know everything? The answer is an emphatic, YES! Go back to my simple example. With my very limited knowledge of hotel entryways, I was able to produce a beautiful hotel entryway. Yes, the AI out-produced what other amateurs who would have designed a hotel entryway without AI. It might even outperform previous non-AI experts. Remember Kasparov? In his chess world, several amateurs working with a powerful computer outperformed a grandmaster. However, think of the power of taking a knowledgeable human and combining that with AI. Experts using AI will outperform non-experts not using AI.

We spoke in detail about learning in the last chapter. I want to revisit it as it relates to expertise. Given that AI knows so much about so many different things, the ability to learn will increase dramatically. This has two effects on expertise. One, gaining expertise will be much faster as you can learn more quickly and target a topic. Two, because learning will accelerate for humans and machines, expertise can disappear much faster. In other words, the path to expertise is shorter than ever—but so is the road to obsolescence. Mastery may come faster—but obsolescence follows just as swiftly if learning stalls.

Think of how this applies to college professors. Most individuals must go through many years of school to become a professor. Once they are granted their Ph.D., they are supposed to be experts in their field. However, with knowledge changing so quickly, that Ph.D. "expert" will only last for a short amount of time if the professor does not diligently continue to learn. And combining our previous thoughts, on their own, they will likely never be as expert as Symbio, the team full of humans and computers working together.

To be an expert in the AI world, learn how to learn and love it because you will have to be continually learning to be an expert in the AI age.

I have one word of warning. The expertise mindset of the AI age will also require a lot more humility, which might be very hard for the current human experts. I'll explain this from my personal perspective.

To become a professor, I spent years in school studying and refining my skills. After I earned my Ph.D., I further refined my abilities through even more years of rigorous academic research. I developed a measure of expertise. Once I developed a measure of expertise, different regulators, business leaders, and other academics sought me out for advice. Having someone else want to know what you think on a topic is a major ego boost. Well, a new accounting professor, Symbio, comes along and in a few short months, Symbio is more expert in every dimension than my expertise. I am completely replaced as an expert. That's a pretty big humble pill to swallow.

I certainly can continue to be an expert if I choose to embrace AI and create my own team of humans and AI agents so that together, we are experts. But to do that, I must admit that I need help from both a computer and other humans. I must admit that by myself, I am not enough. That will take some serious humility.

Because of this challenge, you will likely see some "past-experts" rail against AI and try to turn the world back to how it was before AI was released, so they can still be considered experts. For these "past-experts," it's going to be hard to believe that a Symbio, especially one made of amateurs, can be more expert than them. That might look like a faculty member banning the use of GenAI in the classroom rather than embracing it, regulators restricting AI-assisted medical diagnostics despite its proven accuracy, or seasoned lawyers dismissing AI-driven legal research even when it outperforms human counterparts. It could be a journalist rejecting AI-generated investigative reports or a veteran architect refusing to use AI-assisted design tools that streamline complex structural calculations. In every field, there will be those who resist, clinging to the belief that expertise must come only through the traditional paths they once mastered. But as history has shown, expertise evolves—and those who fail to adapt risk being left behind.

Let's summarize the ground we have covered on expertise. The AI age redefines expertise from individual mastery to AI-assisted collaboration. In the past, expertise was built through years of study and experience, but now, AI enables faster learning and decision-making. Knowledge alone is no longer enough—true expertise lies in applying AI-driven insights effectively. Expertise is now team-based, with AI and humans working together as integrated systems. Traditional experts must embrace humility, as AI allows amateurs to outperform professionals in an increasing number of areas. The ability to adapt, collaborate, and continuously learn is now more important than static knowledge or credentials.

> *Those who resist AI risk becoming obsolete, while those who leverage it can expand their capabilities and shape the future of expertise. In this new world, success is no longer about just what you know but how well you use AI to apply, adapt, and innovate.*

I include the following table to contrast the old and new mindsets.

Scenario	Old Mindset	New GenAI Mindset
Definition of Expertise	Expertise is deep individual knowledge built over years of study and practice.	Expertise is about applying knowledge effectively in collaboration with AI and teams.
How Experts Work	Experts work alone or in hierarchical teams, where knowledge is passed down through experience.	Experts work as part of AI-human teams, leveraging AI agents to enhance decision-making.
Role of Knowledge	Being an expert means having vast amounts of knowledge in a specific domain.	AI provides near-universal knowledge—true expertise lies in applying it wisely.
Speed of Learning	Mastery takes years of study and experience, making expertise exclusive to those with formal training.	AI accelerates learning—anyone can gain expertise faster with the right tools.

Scenario	Old Mindset	New GenAI Mindset
How Expertise is Maintained	Once expertise is achieved, it remains relatively stable over a lifetime.	Expertise must constantly evolve—AI and knowledge change too quickly to rely on past credentials.
Who Can Be an Expert?	Only those with formal education, credentials, and years of experience can be true experts.	Amateurs using AI effectively may outperform traditional experts—expertise is now more democratized.
Attitude Toward AI Assistance	Relying on AI for expertise is cheating or diminishes personal skill.	AI is a necessary partner—embracing it leads to better results than working alone.
Future of Expertise	Traditional experts will always be the best in their field.	AI-human collaboration (AI-centaurs) will outperform even the best individual experts.
Response to AI Disrupting an Expert's Field	Pre-AI experts may resist AI, fearing it will replace them or devalue their skills.	AI experts embrace AI, using it to extend their capabilities and stay ahead.

CHAPTER 8

Perfect is the
Enemy of Good

T he quote 'Perfect is the enemy of good,' first penned by the French philosopher Voltaire in 1772, is an important reminder of the dangers of perfectionism—a mindset that has persisted across centuries and cultures. Perfectionism has positive and negative aspects. The idea of trying to do your best at a task is highly valuable and a noble mindset. The downside of perfectionism is that it hyper-focuses on the word 'best,' not allowing an individual to accept outcomes or processes that are moving in the right direction but not yet 'perfect.'

A perfectionist mentality can have significant drawbacks in the world of AI. Remember the chapter on how GenAI works; it's probabilistic. This probability means that GenAI will sometimes make mistakes and not produce perfect answers. For some tasks, mistakes may be made even in the future when better models are released. GenAI is not perfect in a deterministic sense, and likely never will be.

I've seen how the perfectionist mindset holds back individuals first exposed to GenAI. When I train employees of companies, there is invariably someone in the room who says something like, "I tried [pick your GenAI tool] to do X, and it failed. This technology is overhyped and worthless!"

I'm used to these types of comments in my presentations, and I'm fully prepared to talk about them. It is important to note that the person is right. GenAI failed them. The person is also wrong. Just because GenAI failed once doesn't mean it will fail every time. This type of generalization is typical of the perfectionist attitude— because it isn't perfect, now, it is worthless. This is why perfectionism can be so crippling. It leaves no room for growth— it demands perfection, and it demands it now!

In these situations, I will often point out a few things to the frustrated employee. First, the person often uses a free or older version of a GenAI model that is less capable than the latest model. Thus, while they think that GenAI failed them, it is really that the version they were using failed them.

Second, remember back to our discussion of the "jagged technological frontier" in a previous chapter. GenAI is advancing in a "jagged" and not linear way. Often, the employee tried something months ago and doesn't realize the technology has since evolved—now integrating tools like code generation or up-to-date data access—that make old things now possible.

Third, many users haven't moved beyond a surface-level understanding of how to use GenAI effectively. While the tools are intuitive to access, using them well—really well—requires skill, strategy, and deliberate practice. Just like any powerful technology, results depend heavily on how you use it. If your experience with GenAI has been disappointing, it's worth asking: have you taken the time to learn how to prompt, iterate, and collaborate with it properly? In some cases, it's not that the AI failed—it's that the user never truly learned to use it.

Finally, I call into question the idea that because it didn't do the task perfectly, does that really mean it is worthless for all tasks and shouldn't be learned? Clearly, that answer is no. One needs to learn how and when to use it. It is not the solution to everything, but it can help. Progress towards perfection can be valuable, even if something is not perfect…yet.

More often, these comments are subtler than the dramatic examples I mentioned earlier, such as "I asked the AI to generate a marketing email, but it didn't exactly match our brand voice, so I had to rewrite most of it. It's just not worth the effort." Or, "I tried using it to summarize a legal document, but it missed some important details. If I must double-check everything, what's the point?" Or, my favorite, "That's just not how I do it. It doesn't do it my way."

Notice in these comments the same theme that because GenAI didn't do the task perfectly, it must be of little value. Just like perfectionism has some seeds of truth (e.g., doing a good job is the goal), these comments have seeds of truth. GenAI tools often will not create a perfect match with tone. They may also miss some details. This technology is not perfect. However, the change of mindset that is needed is that even though they are not perfect, they can still be helpful. Let's take a brief detour into the history of driverless cars.

Driverless cars, or fully autonomous vehicles, are vehicles that can operate without human intervention by utilizing a combination of sensors and AI to navigate and respond to their environment safely. The journey toward fully autonomous vehicles offers a powerful parallel to our experience with GenAI. In the early 2000s, the Defense Advanced Research Projects Agency (DARPA) organized a series of races—most famously, the DARPA Grand Challenge—that pushed the limits of driverless technology in harsh desert environments. The competition required autonomous vehicles to navigate a 150-mile route through the Mojave Desert. The competitor that finished the race first would win one million dollars.

Twenty-one entrants had to pass a one-mile obstacle course to make it into the final race. Seven teams were able to complete this preliminary race, and eight others were deemed to have done "good enough" to be entered in the final 150-mile race.

On March 13, 2004, the teams gathered to race for the one-million-dollar prize. Well, most of the teams gathered because two more teams withdrew before even starting. The race was planned to take ten hours, but after three hours, only four vehicles were even operational, and the rest didn't survive much longer. At the end of the day, no vehicle finished the race. In fact, the vehicle that went the furthest only traveled 7.4 miles. In terms of winning or even completing the race, every team was a complete failure.

Ending the story there would miss the key reason I'm sharing it—something can fail initially and still go on to be astonishingly successful. In the case of driverless cars, just one year later, in 2005, teams refined their designs and algorithms and returned to race a slightly different course. On October 8, 2005, 23 finalists again attempted the competition. This time the race was set for a 132-mile course that involved driving through three narrow tunnels, more than 100 sharp turns, and finishing by driving over Beer Bottle Pass, a mountain pass with a steep rock face on one side and a sheer drop off on the other. While in 2004, no car made it more than 7.4 miles, in 2005, five teams completed the entire race.

The story of driverless cars still isn't over. The DARPA grand challenge continued in 2007, but the challenge was moved to an urban environment. Autonomous vehicles had to complete a 60-mile course in less than six hours and obey all traffic regulations, while also performing normal driving tasks like merging into traffic. Six teams successfully completed this race.

Although some cars completed the 2007 challenge in more real-world conditions, driverless cars were still not mainstream. The successful results did cause the press to start hyping this technology with discussions of the imminent complete change of the world. Stories about how traffic jams would cease to exist, parking lots would all be developed into new buildings, and how we would see the end of driving jobs, like long-haul truckers, started to emerge. The press started presenting this "perfect world" that would exist. Obviously, at the time of this writing, that world still doesn't exist.

What lessons do we learn, and are continuing to learn, from the history of driverless cars? Imagine how a perfectionist—let's call him Bob—might interpret the development of self-driving cars. Let's take a peek inside Bob's mind.

2004: The Disaster

Well, that was an absolute joke. Not a single car finished. Not even close! The best one only made it a measly 7.4 miles, and the whole race was supposed to be 150 miles. What a waste of time and money. I knew this was a pipe dream. The idea that a computer could drive a car better than a human? Ridiculous. These researchers can keep throwing money at this, but it's never going to work. I mean, if a human driver only made it 7.4 miles in a race, they'd be laughed off the road. Why should we expect anything better from a machine?

2005: A Few Lucky Wins?

Alright, so they made some improvements. A few cars actually finished the course this time. Big deal. This was still a closed course. No pedestrians, no cyclists, no real traffic. They set everything up in perfect conditions, and even then, most of the teams still failed. That's the part people aren't talking about—most of them still couldn't do it! And even the "successful" ones, what do they really prove? Under controlled conditions, a few cars stumble their way to the finish line. That doesn't mean anything in the real world. These things will never handle rush hour traffic, snow, construction zones, or the guy who cuts you off without signaling. Wake me up when one of these things can handle the chaos of city driving.

2007: Moving the Goalposts

So now they've got a few cars driving in an "urban environment." But let's be real—this is just another setup. It's a controlled course. They're still picking the conditions. They say the cars had to obey traffic laws, merge into traffic, and drive like a human would, but they still had a ton of limitations. What happens when a kid runs into the street chasing a ball? What about a driver who waves you in when there's no stop sign? What about an unmarked construction zone with confusing detours? A human can react to all of that instinctively. A computer? No chance.

And yet, the media is already acting like self-driving cars are just around the corner. They're talking about a world with no traffic jams, no parking lots, and no truck drivers. Are they serious? We're nowhere close! Just because a handful of cars managed to complete a pre-planned course doesn't mean we're about to eliminate human drivers. This is classic overhype. I give it another five years before people realize this is never going to work.

Leaving Bob's mind, let's analyze his mindset. The first thing to notice is Bob is right at every individual point in time. The cars didn't finish in 2004. Most cars still failed in 2005 in ideal circumstances. The 2007 race didn't herald the triumph of driverless cars. That's the persistent challenge with a perfectionist mindset—it often feels right in the moment.

However, what Bob failed to see because of his perfectionist mindset was the tremendous progress over time and the benefits that accumulated along the way. With a growth mindset, a person, let's call her Cindy, would look at this same story and see how much progress was made in just a few short years and that the trajectory is very encouraging. Also, Cindy would recognize the benefits that accrued along the way. So even though driverless cars are not ubiquitous, they helped spur other technological innovations already having significant impacts on driving, such as advanced driver assistance systems that include things like automatic emergency braking, lane departure warnings, adaptive cruise control, and self-parking.

While not fully autonomous driving, these features developed largely because of work on building self-driving cars. Also, Cindy can see the other secondary developments such as the development of ultra-precise mapping technology, improvements in LIDAR (light detection and ranging) technology, vehicle-to-everything computing (vehicles talk to infrastructure like traffic lights), and navigation technology for other tasks like warehouse automation that result from the development of driverless cars.

Let's finish the driverless car discussion by talking about what exists as of the writing of this book. Although driverless technology hasn't disrupted all driving, it is a growing sector and has been employed in the real world. For instance, you can now use a driverless taxi in cities like Los Angeles, San Francisco, Phoenix, Miami, Atlanta, and Austin, to name a few. There is now enough data to make meaningful, real-world comparisons about how self-driving cars compare to humans. Here is data from Waymo, a self-driving car company, based on more than seven million miles driven by their driverless cars.

According to the 2023 data, self-driving cars operating in Phoenix, San Francisco, and Los Angeles reported an any-injury-reported crash rate of 0.6 incidents per million miles (IPMM), compared to 2.80 IPMM for human drivers. This represents an 80% reduction in injury-related crashes, showing that autonomous vehicles significantly lower the risk of injury compared to human-operated vehicles. Furthermore, the police-reported crash rate for self-driving vehicles was 2.1 IPMM, while human-driven vehicles had a rate of 4.68 IPMM. This marks a 55% reduction in police-reported crashes, with human drivers experiencing 2.2 times more crashes than autonomous vehicles.

However, when evaluating crashes involving any property damage or injury, the results were more varied. While some comparisons showed statistically significant reductions, others did not, indicating that additional research and data collection are needed to fully understand the impact of self-driving cars in these scenarios. Overall, these statistics strongly suggest that self-driving technology can significantly reduce crash rates, making roads safer compared to human-driven vehicles.

Let's recap the lessons learned from driverless cars and how they apply to GenAI:

- **Early Failures Do Not Mean Ultimate Failure** – The 2004 DARPA Grand Challenge was a complete failure, with no car finishing the race. A perfectionist mindset would have dismissed autonomous vehicles as impossible. However, failure was just the first step in learning and improving—a key lesson for shifting away from perfectionism.

- **Incremental Progress is Still Progress** – By 2005, multiple teams successfully completed the course, proving that technology improves through iteration. Perfectionists often see anything less than immediate success as failure, but real innovation comes from refining and improving over time.

- **Success Happens in Stages, Not Instantly** – In 2007, autonomous cars tackled urban driving, a major leap from previous tests. Perfectionists might have still called the technology inadequate because it wasn't fully self-sufficient, but those with a growth mindset saw that each step forward was meaningful.

- **Perfectionist Thinking Can Blind Us to Long-Term Progress** – At each stage, a perfectionist might have focused on what self-driving cars *couldn't* do rather than what they *could* do. This narrow focus on flaws rather than progress prevents appreciation for meaningful advancements—whether in AI, self-driving technology, or personal growth.

- **Imperfect Technologies Can Still Offer Great Value** – Even though fully autonomous vehicles are not yet the norm, self-driving research has led to widespread safety innovations. Similarly, GenAI doesn't have to be perfect to be useful—it can still enhance productivity, creativity, and efficiency despite occasional flaws.

- **Adopting a Growth Mindset Enables Future Success** – If researchers had abandoned self-driving technology after early failures, today's progress wouldn't exist. The same is true for GenAI—embracing its current capabilities while recognizing its future potential is far more productive than dismissing it for not being perfect yet.

> *Perfectionism focuses on what isn't working, while a growth mindset recognizes potential and progress. Just like self-driving technology, GenAI is evolving, and those who learn to work with its imperfections will benefit the most.*

I have noticed one additional tendency related to GenAI and perfectionism. People very frequently hold GenAI to a higher standard than they do humans. Hearkening back to the chapter on deterministic and probabilistic thinking, many people expect GenAI to be perfect, whereas they expect only humans to be at some level of good. In the example of driverless cars, this can be seen by people not wanting driverless taxis until they have no accidents, even though current humans can't drive at that level. The reality is that if an AI, whether GenAI or driverless cars, is better than a human, we should be willing to use it, even if it is not perfect. GenAI will make mistakes, but if it makes fewer mistakes than humans, we should embrace its use, since it produces higher-quality outcomes than human decisions.

Watch what happens when we apply this mindset to the examples of the marketing email that didn't match the brand voice or the legal summarization that missed a few important details. The response to these individuals should acknowledge that the GenAI tool was not perfect. The question of whether it should be used should compare the GenAI not to perfection, but rather to what a human would do. If GenAI isn't faster or more accurate than a human, don't use it—at least not yet—but if it is faster and produces better output than a human, even if it is not perfect, you should encourage its use.

Here are the key takeaways to help you shift from a perfectionist to a growth-oriented GenAI mindset.

Scenario	Old Mindset	New GenAI Mindset
Early Failures in AI Adoption	If AI makes mistakes, it is unreliable and unusable.	AI will improve over time; errors are part of the learning process.
Incremental AI Progress	If AI isn't perfect now, it will never be good enough.	AI is evolving rapidly—small improvements lead to major breakthroughs.
AI in Workplace Tasks	AI-generated content isn't perfect, so it's not useful.	AI can increase efficiency and reduce workload, even if minor revisions are needed.
Expectations for Innovation	New technology must deliver perfection immediately.	True innovation happens through iterations and improvements over time.
AI versus Human Performance	If AI gets something wrong, it should be abandoned.	AI should be compared to human performance, not perfection.

CHAPTER 9

The Hidden Bias in AI:
Who Decides What's "Right"?

For years, we've trusted our computers to work like flawless calculators—objective, impartial, and free of human quirks. I still remember one of the first times I introduced AI to a group; someone asked, "Aren't AI models biased?" That simple question struck at the very core of the issue. It forced us to consider the fact that AI isn't some all-knowing authority dishing out pure, unvarnished truth. Instead, it's a reflection of the data and human decisions that went into its creation and prompting, complete with all the imperfections that come along.

When we talk about bias, it helps to understand that the term means different things depending on the context. In everyday conversation, bias usually suggests an unfair preference—a kind of prejudice where one option is favored over another without good reason. For instance, think about sports. Have you ever watched a game with someone who is a fan of the rival team? Whenever the ref makes a call it is obvious the ref is biased for or against your team. I might yell at the screen, "Are you blind that was a foul! Why are you always against my team!" while your friend retorts, "Finally they aren't favoring your team, and they are calling the game correctly!" Both you and your friend think the ref is biased in that she favors the other side unfairly.

In activities outside of sports, we talk about all kinds of biases, including bias based on age, gender, race, or other categories. Implicit in the conversational use of bias is the idea of something being wrong. You should pay both those people the same or else you are biased, meaning that you are doing something unethical or immoral. In contrast, in the world of statistics, bias is defined in a much more neutral way. It refers to a systematic deviation from a true value. If a survey only reaches one segment of the population, the resulting data might be skewed—but that skew isn't inherently "bad;" it's just a predictable error given the methodology. For example, if I try and predict a presidential election and I only survey people in states that vote heavily in favor of a particular candidate, my results will be biased, but that doesn't necessarily imply any moral or ethical wrongdoing. In essence, the common understanding of bias carries moral weight, whereas statistical bias is simply a technical term for a deviation from a true value.

Another example is the data on job roles. Current statistics show that nearly 98% of nursery nurses are women, while about 93% of window cleaners are men. Viewed through the lens of everyday language, many would immediately conclude that something is wrong—an unfair imbalance that needs correcting. Yet, from a statistical perspective, if those numbers accurately reflect a workforce gathered from properly collected data, then there's no bias in the results at all; the numbers simply mirror reality.

This example highlights a critical decision point when developing an AI model. If we train a model to reflect raw data—such as the observed gender distributions in various professions—it will faithfully reproduce those statistics. If I ask an AI model that is only trained on real-world data to make an image of a window cleaner, it will almost always make the image of a male, since the training data likely represents window cleaners as male the vast majority of the time. In this case, the model will be considered biased from common-day usage of the term, but unbiased from a statistical use of the term.

In contrast, if we want a model that meets our cultural or moral expectations of fairness, we must step in during training or fine-tuning to adjust those imbalances. In the job example, if we believe that window-washers should be depicted as 50% male and 50% female, then we have to alter the model accordingly, since it won't perform this way based on real-world training data. In this case, the model would appear unbiased in the everyday sense, but statistically, it would be biased.

This example highlights the major challenge of GenAI related to bias: you simply can't have it both ways. You must choose whether you want the model to produce outputs that are based on moral judgments or that are based on the statistical analysis of the results. The choice is deliberate, underscoring the inherent trade-offs in creating an AI that is simultaneously statistically accurate and culturally balanced.

This duality in the meaning of bias becomes even more important when we consider how AI works. When an AI model is trained on massive datasets—ranging from books and websites to social media posts—it absorbs the full spectrum of human ideas, including both our greatest achievements and the messiest parts of human nature. Human minds have produced amazing literature and art but have also generated harmful, discriminatory content. Statistically speaking, if the model simply reflects the patterns it has seen, then it is unbiased in that technical sense. But that doesn't mean the output is free from the everyday kind of bias many of us find objectionable.

For instance, imagine an AI asked to write a profile of a job candidate. If the training data is dominated by narratives that associate youth with innovation and depict older workers as less adaptable, the resulting profile might emphasize stereotypes about age. To a data scientist trying to design a model to match the training data, that's exactly what the numbers should produce, but to someone expecting a balanced, fair portrayal, it might feel skewed or even discriminatory.

It isn't just about where the AI gets its information—it's also about how developers choose to shape that information after the initial training phase. As a reminder from the chapter explaining how AI works, once the raw model is built, there's a stage called fine-tuning, where developers adjust the model's behavior based on what they consider acceptable or desirable. Fine-tuning is like adjusting the seasoning in a dish—small changes can greatly affect the final result. For example, if a model is fine-tuned to be more sensitive to issues of representation, developers might deliberately adjust its outputs to show more diverse perspectives—even if that means deviating from the historical or statistical norm.

Consider a real-world case that provides a striking example of this tension involving Alphabet, the parent company of Google. In early 2024, Alphabet introduced a feature within its AI Gemini chatbot that allowed users to generate images of historical figures. When prompted to create depictions of America's Founding Fathers, many users were surprised to see images that included women and people of color—even though historically speaking, America's Founding Fathers were white men. Critics quickly accused Google of rewriting history, of imposing modern diversity ideals onto a group that, by every historical account, was not diverse at all. Google eventually admitted that the AI "missed the mark" and paused the feature to make adjustments. Google's engineers had chosen to fine-tune their model to focus on representation, which caused it to deviate from historically accepted facts.

These examples raise an essential question: What should we expect from our AI? Should it strictly mirror the data it's given, even if that data is a patchwork of human error and subjectivity? Or should it be fine-tuned to align with modern values, even if that means distorting historical or statistical truths? There isn't an easy answer here. The term "bias" itself becomes a moving target—it can denote a neutral, technical phenomenon or serve as a loaded critique of unfairness, depending on who's doing the judging.

This question is even more challenging because if you select that the model should behave according to some modern values, you have to decide which values to implement for fine-tuning. An example of this is the GenAI model developed by DeepSeek. DeepSeek is a Chinese AI company that has produced several large language models. The models caused major disruption when they were released because they were less expensive to operate. As people started using the models, however, they started to notice that the company had designed the models so that they would not discuss controversial historical Chinese events. Instead, the model will just report it can't discuss that issue.

One of the largest challenges of this choice by model builders is that it is not made transparent to the user. So, while a user has the mindset that the model is operating in a statistically unbiased manner, it may actually be designed to represent certain moral norms. Or the user could be expecting the model to output based on certain moral norms, but the model is actually trying to be statistically unbiased.

Given that most users won't know whether a model prioritizes statistical accuracy or moral fairness, how should we interact with these systems? At a high level, as users, we can advocate for policies that require more disclosure and transparency around model training data and fine-tuning so we can be educated about the choices that went into building the models. Knowing how the models will likely react will help us know how to use them. On a day-to-day basis, we will have to adjust our mindset to both accept and question output at the same time. How do you do this?

Instead of viewing AI as an all-knowing, objective authority, we need to treat it as a collaborative partner shaped by human input. When an AI produces a response, it isn't handing us a finished product but rather a starting point—a draft shaped by the interplay of its training data and the choices made during fine-tuning. Importantly, it is also shaped by the prompt. If you receive an answer that feels one-dimensional or oddly skewed, don't just accept it at face value. Instead, challenge it. Ask follow-up questions, rephrase your prompt, or request alternative viewpoints.

For instance, if I ask for a prompt of an image of a nurse, most models will return a nurse depicted as a woman because of their training data, which very likely represents most nurses as women. If I don't want an image of a female nurse, I can change my prompt to ask for a male nurse. In this way, the model will still produce what I want. If the model still doesn't produce what I want after I have changed my prompt, I can choose to use a different model.

To shift our mindset about AI bias, we must stop assuming that AI is neutral or infallible. Instead, we must recognize that AI reflects human decisions—both in the data it learns from and the fine-tuning choices made by developers. A more effective mindset is to see AI as a tool that, like humans, has perspectives shaped by its experiences (training data) and influences (fine-tuning). This means approaching AI-generated content with curiosity rather than blind trust—questioning outputs, seeking alternative viewpoints, and refining prompts to uncover biases and gaps. Instead of expecting AI to be perfectly objective, we should acknowledge that bias is a trade-off rather than a defect, requiring deliberate choices about fairness and accuracy.

This table summarizes our changing mindset around bias.

Scenario	Old Mindset	New GenAI Mindset
AI Objectivity	AI is neutral and unbiased, providing purely factual information.	AI reflects the biases of its training data and developer choices—its outputs must be evaluated critically.
Bias Perception	Bias in AI is always bad and should be eliminated.	Bias is inevitable and must be managed—decisions about fairness and accuracy require trade-offs.
Interacting with AI Outputs	AI responses are final and authoritative.	AI responses are starting points—question, refine, and challenge them to get the best results.
Transparency Expectations	AI should be trusted without needing to understand how it was built.	Demand transparency in AI development and fine-tuning to make informed usage decisions.
Adapting to AI Limitations	If AI produces biased or flawed responses, it's unreliable.	Adjust prompts, explore alternative models, and refine approaches to mitigate bias and improve results.
Role of AI in Society	AI should be completely fair and free of human influence.	AI will always reflect human values in some way—our role is to guide and oversee it responsibly.

CHAPTER 10

AI Gone Wrong:
The Risks We Need to Prepare For

Most of the examples in this book have been positives about GenAI. I stand by those positives. We need to update our mindsets for a new AI world. That said, the book would not be complete without discussing some of the risks and negatives that exist and how these should be carefully incorporated into our mindsets when living in an AI world. This is not a comprehensive list, but it highlights a few dangers worth incorporating into our mindset.

Let's start at the beginning of the book when I explained how GenAI is probabilistic and not deterministic and, thus, can hallucinate. As a reminder, a hallucination is when a GenAI tool reports factually incorrect information as true. Although not mentioned in every chapter, hallucinations are a risk to consider whenever you use GenAI. I'll give just a couple of examples.

Think back to the chapter on expertise and the chapter on learning. In both chapters, hallucinations are a big problem. You can't be an expert if you are factually incorrect. You aren't learning productively if what you are learning is wrong. When using GenAI, I feel like my brain is accurately portrayed by the Disney movie *Inside-Out*. In this movie, there are five different emotions in the main character Riley's brain: joy, sadness, fear, anger, and disgust, each of which is represented by a different character. Each character can create memories. When the girl is young, all her memories are a single emotion. Still, one of the main messages of the movie is that as you get older, memories can combine emotions, and memories can evoke, for example, both joy and sadness.

When I started working with GenAI, I had a single-emotion mindset. The GenAI was either good or bad, useful or worthless. Over time and experience working with the tool, my mindset has changed to a more nuanced understanding of the tool, especially around hallucinations. To succeed with GenAI, I must be skeptical and trusting of the output every time I use it. This is one reason why domain knowledge is so important. In previous chapters, I never claimed learning is obsolete just because AI knows a lot. As I gain knowledge about a topic, I can better discern when GenAI is hallucinating and when it is not. This helps me use GenAI more effectively.

This dual, trusting-skeptic mindset has also helped me learn some tricks to working with hallucinations. Through trial and error, I have discovered strategies to mitigate the risks of hallucinations.

First, I use GenAI most for brainstorming rather than relying on it for hard facts. I request references or verify the details independently when I need specific factual information. I often write a piece myself before using GenAI to refine and improve it. In cases where accuracy is critical, I cross-check the output by using another AI or running fact-checking prompts in a separate conversation before manually checking them myself. Additionally, I have found it useful to instruct the AI to acknowledge uncertainty rather than generate misleading information. For instance, I might ask GenAI to "List all the risks in this setting," but then I will add, "but if there are no risks, state there are no risks." By incorporating these techniques, I can harness the power of GenAI while reducing hallucination risks, allowing me to use the tool more effectively and responsibly. Even with precautions, I still maintain a trusting-skeptic mindset when reviewing anything produced with GenAI.

Beyond hallucinations, GenAI can be used for fundamentally evil purposes. These tools have been used to create content that is illegal and immoral. It is not worth even worth listing the most harmful or offensive uses. GenAI can be used for other illegal activities like automating hacking and scanning computer systems for vulnerabilities. I categorize all these types of AI use as categorically evil. As the human race, we need to come together to discuss how to eliminate these types of uses.

There are other uses that can be both nefarious and positive, like deepfake technology. Deepfakes use AI to generate realistic-looking but fabricated images, videos, or audio that mimic real people or events. Deepfake tools are increasingly available and easy to use. Some tools can take a single photo of a person and a short audio file, allowing the user to make the person say anything you want in video form.

Before talking about the negatives of deepfakes, there are some positives to consider. After giving a presentation to a group of professors, one of the professors came up to visit with me and, in a scratchy, raspy voice, described how his vocal cords had been damaged. He wanted to know if the technology would allow him to create audio files with his undamaged voice. Voice cloning software makes it possible to create audio files for his students and family using his undamaged voice.

I also use a program called Synthesia. This AI program allowed me to film myself and use the trained model to create videos of myself. For teaching students, now, rather than having to film a video multiple times until I get it right, I can type in what I want to say, click publish, and have a perfect video of me teaching my students. This is especially helpful when accounting rules or technology are updated in my field. Rather than film an entirely new video or try to do a "patch" to my first video, I can simply edit and republish the deepfake video of myself. It saves a ton of time and makes it easier to have up-to-date content.

One final positive, using deepfake technology can be fun. You can make funny videos of yourself or be creative in new ways. When used in the right way, this technology can have positives.

Everything I said about deepfakes is true, *but* it can also be abused. In a research study I designed with my coauthors, we created a deepfake video of the CEO of Apple, Tim Cook. We exercised significant care in conducting the study to make sure the video was not released to the public. With this deepfake video, we tested whether this type of media could influence investors and whether traditional ways of detecting fake news that was not deepfaked would solve the problem.

The news isn't good. Our research showed that deepfake video and audio could influence investors, and the traditional ways a user detects non-deepfake fake news were ineffective against realistic deepfakes. I presented this research to employees at the Securities and Exchange Commission (SEC), and we discussed what this means for the markets. I expressed how scary this technology is because detection can be very difficult, especially as the AI models get better.

This technology is also scary because of the difficulty of detecting deepfakes with technology. One of the ways deepfakes are made is to have one model make a deepfake image, video, or audio and a second model try to detect if it is fake. If the computer identifies the creation is fake, the first model tries again. This repeats itself millions of times until the second model can't detect the fake. The real concerning part is that if a smart computer scientist develops a new way to algorithmically detect a deepfake video, that new method can be used as the second model to detect deepfakes until the first model makes creations that the new method cannot detect. This cat-and-mouse game will continue, and at any given time, the technology may favor the ones making the deepfakes and then the ones trying to detect the deepfakes. I warned the SEC that it's going to be very hard to detect all deepfakes and prevent the markets from acting on deepfake news.

It's not just markets that have to worry. I tested a deepfake phishing attack on an organization (I am intentionally keeping the organization's name hidden). A phishing attack is sending an email and asking the user to do something. With permission from the organization, we created a deepfake of the organization's leader. We sent an email asking all the employees to log into a website to update their information. In the message, we included a deepfake voicemail from the leader and were able to fool almost 50% of the employees into clicking on our link. Not only did they click the link, but they also entered their username and password into our fake website.

Our controlled phishing experiment closely mirrors a real-world case. A finance employee at a British engineering firm was deceived into transferring $25 million to fraudsters. During a video conference call, the scammers utilized deepfake technology to impersonate the company's CFO. The employee, seeing and hearing his boss, did what we all do when our boss asks us to do something, he did it. Unfortunately, it wasn't his boss, but rather a deepfake version of his boss, and the company lost the $25 million.

Deepfake technologies are just one risk to businesses. GenAI represents numerous other business risks. If you have an interest in learning more about these risks and what you can do about it, I encourage you to go to http://genai.global/, where my colleagues and I have created a GenAI governance framework you can read to explore this issue more deeply.

So, what are you to do in this new world, where you can't trust what you see or hear? What concerns me most about deepfakes and other GenAI technologies is that we will stop believing everything we hear, and trust will further erode in this world. If public trust collapses, it could lead to complete societal breakdown.

I don't have a solution to this problem. Right now, my best mindset change is to follow the Russian proverb, "Trust, but verify." Like the multi-emotion memories described in Inside Out, we are going to have to combine two seemingly opposite ideas, trust and verify, into a single mindset. This means we might have to try new strategies. For instance, a few companies have told me they now have passwords for certain transactions. If their boss requests an action, they confirm it with a shared password before proceeding. You might need to increase in-person interactions for some decisions. Being aware and discussing what you will do in potentially compromising circumstances is a good start for adjusting your mindset to both trust and verify in the AI world.

Let's move on to another potential risk of GenAI technologies. I raise this concern after observing negatives of social media usage. Ironically, social media was designed to make us more social and make it easier to connect with others, but too often it has the opposite effect and actually make us feel more isolated and alone. The same concern could exist from the development of GenAI.

After the release of ChatGPT, a company scraped a large portion of the Internet to find out how people were actually using ChatGPT. They published the top 100 use cases, which is a wonderful list to help you think about unique ways to use this technology (search for the Harvard Business Review article "How People are Really Using GenAI" to see the complete list). What struck me the most when I read the list was the number two use of GenAI: "therapy/companionship." When the study was updated in 2025, "therapy/companionship" had moved into the number one position for use of GenAI.

You can download many apps that allow you to have an AI friend to talk to or even a girlfriend or boyfriend with whom you can share an emotional attachment. ChatGPT has a voice mode and even digital home assistants, like Alexa, are now enabled with GenAI-like technology. This makes it effortless to talk to an AI at any time. Will this create similar, or even greater, problems as with social media? Will a group of people turn to AI to be their friends, depriving them of human interaction and friendship? If so, how large of a group will that be, and what will be the consequences?

AI could dehumanize us, encouraging machine-like behavior over authentic human connection. We must actively push against this tendency and instead use AI to make us more human. We must avoid the mindset that an AI algorithm is better than a human for a relationship. Yes, it is easier and less demanding as a relationship partner. Still, the long-term costs of giving into that easier mindset will be similar to or greater destruction than we have seen from social media in real-world relationships.

There is hope that AI can be used to enhance human interaction. We conducted a research study with nearly 2,000 accounting interns using AI to enhance their social skills. Although most people stereotype accountants as being antisocial, back-office workers, a great deal of accounting work is human-related. Consider auditors who make sure companies report their finances correctly. A large part of auditors' work is to interview other people. Prior research shows that especially new auditors, often face significant anxiety in talking to people of a different rank— think having a new staff person talk to a senior leader of a company she is auditing.

We wondered if we could use AI to help overcome this anxiety, this negative mindset. We designed training to teach interns how to interact as auditors, and then we had them practice interacting with an AI bot that was trained to act like a business professional. We found that just having an intern go through one hour of training and practice with an AI, significantly decreased their anxiety to interact with a more senior person. So, while AI has the potential to cause social problems, if used correctly, it can also be part of the solution to help improve social problems. We will have to carefully adapt to how we use this tool.

Finally, I raise the significant risk of "more is less." This concept of "more is less" refers to the paradoxical situation where increased productivity driven by AI leads not necessarily to greater satisfaction or improved quality of life, but rather to a feeling of being overwhelmed, burned out, and ultimately less fulfilled. The challenge arises from the pressure to consistently produce more content, analyses, or innovations—and, importantly, to ensure this increased quantity maintains high quality or even increases in quality. For instance, AI-driven tools can now help an employee generate ten times the volume of detailed reports, compelling articles, or sophisticated analyses compared to just a few years ago. While initially appearing advantageous, the combined pressure for quantity and sustained high quality creates a significant mental and emotional strain.

The pressure to constantly produce both more and better aligns closely with the psychological concept of the Hedonic Treadmill (also known as Hedonic Adaptation), which suggests that humans quickly return to a baseline level of happiness despite significant positive or negative changes in life circumstances. Initially, improved productivity can feel exhilarating, bringing recognition and satisfaction. However, as these heightened expectations become the new normal, any incremental gains in output or quality no longer bring sustained satisfaction or happiness. Instead, employees find themselves trapped on a treadmill of perpetual dissatisfaction and stress, constantly striving for more without experiencing lasting fulfillment.

An example from literature that demonstrates this risk is the character of Jay Gatsby in F. Scott Fitzgerald's *The Great Gatsby*. Gatsby continually achieves more—more wealth, more lavish parties, more social recognition—yet never attains the lasting happiness he seeks. Each new achievement quickly becomes insufficient, propelling him to relentlessly chase further accomplishments, ultimately leaving him feeling empty and dissatisfied.

Moreover, this productivity-driven environment risks organizations undervaluing their human employees, creating an atmosphere of job insecurity. If business leaders adopt a mindset viewing AI as capable of performing most tasks faster and cheaper, employees may internalize fears of replaceability. This perception—accurate or not—can lead to widespread anxiety, lower morale, and decreased loyalty, ironically creating an environment where individuals feel less human and more machine-like.

Organizations have a significant role to play in addressing the "more is less" risk. First, organizations must consciously redefine success by emphasizing qualities uniquely human—empathy, kindness, ethical judgment—and clearly delineate responsibilities where humans excel versus tasks best handled by AI. This approach might look like a tech company deliberately crafting job descriptions emphasizing human strengths, making it clear to employees why their judgment and empathy mattered despite heavy AI integration.

Additionally, organizations need to actively consider the psychological well-being of employees and avoid the temptation to treat their humans as AI algorithms. This can be very difficult because the AI employees don't struggle from the more-is-less risk; but it is critically important to keep humans happy and engaged at work. Reward and recognition systems might help in this regard if they evolve beyond numeric or financial targets toward celebrating meaningful human contributions. Imagine recognition awards specifically designed to celebrate impactful actions in mentoring, collaboration, and social impact.

Regardless of whether your organization takes steps to manage this risk, you can make personal choices to avoid the more-is-less trap. You can proactively redefine personal success by prioritizing tasks aligned with intrinsic meaning and impact rather than external recognition alone. This might mean choosing to work for an organization with a mission you believe in or reframing your work around what you do that has intrinsic meaning.

One way to reframe your work is to engage in what positive psychologists call job crafting. A specific form of job crafting, known as cognitive crafting, involves reframing how you perceive your job, making it feel more purposeful and fulfilling. Research shows that hospital janitors who shift their perspective from simply cleaning floors, emptying trash bins, and disinfecting surfaces to seeing their role as actively contributing to patient healing by maintaining a safe, clean, and comforting environment experience higher job satisfaction and engagement. By changing how you view your work, you can enhance intrinsic motivation and avoid feeling like a cog in the system.

Practicing mindful disengagement is another powerful strategy to avoid the trap of constant productivity pressure. This might involve setting firm boundaries around work hours, engaging in activities purely for enjoyment, or taking deliberate "tech breaks." Additionally, cultivating habits of regular reflection and gratitude can interrupt the Hedonic Treadmill, helping individuals appreciate incremental successes rather than perpetually chasing more. A colleague recently adopted journaling to record daily achievements—however small—and found this approach profoundly improved his sense of fulfillment and resilience against burnout.

In summary, navigating the AI-driven "more is less" paradox requires intentional organizational and individual mindset changes. By fostering cultures that emphasize psychological safety, human value, and meaningful contributions, alongside individual strategies that resist perpetual adaptation pressures, we can harness the power of GenAI without sacrificing our humanity or enduring unnecessary stress and dissatisfaction.

Generative AI presents significant opportunities, yet it also brings considerable risks, such as hallucinations, deepfakes, erosion of social connections, and the challenging "more is less" productivity paradox. Successfully navigating these complexities requires intentionally cultivating adaptive mindsets, especially the critical "trust but verify" approach. Embracing this dual mindset helps users responsibly manage AI outputs, identify inaccuracies, and maintain informed skepticism. Additionally, practical safeguards, enhanced human oversight, and proactive awareness of AI's broader social and psychological impacts are essential. Ultimately, by prioritizing human-centric values, ethical vigilance, and psychological well-being, we can harness AI's vast potential without losing our humanity or compromising our social and emotional health.

As with the other chapters, I summarize in table form a few ways your mindset needs should change in the AI world.

Scenario	Old Mindset	New GenAI Mindset
AI Accuracy	AI provides correct, definitive answers.	AI outputs can be incorrect; verify accuracy independently.
Malicious AI Uses	AI risks are rare or overstated; minimal precautions are needed.	AI can easily be misused; proactive safeguards and vigilance are necessary.
Deepfake Risks	Deepfakes are purely harmful; avoid at all costs.	Deepfakes have beneficial uses but must be handled with extreme caution.
AI and Social Interaction	AI interaction is harmless entertainment.	AI interaction risks real-world social isolation; balance is critical.
Productivity and Well-being	More output means better results and satisfaction.	Increased output may lead to burnout; prioritize sustainable productivity and human value.
Trust in AI Outputs	AI outputs should be accepted at face value.	"Trust but verify"—always critically evaluate and cross-check AI outputs.

CHAPTER 11

Changing and Sustaining
Your New AI Mindsets

T hus far, we've explored how important it is to update our mindsets for a rapidly evolving AI future. We've looked at the importance of creativity over retrieval, the difference between deterministic and probabilistic thinking, and how embracing AI can supercharge—even redefine—human expertise. Yet knowing what mindsets to adopt is only half the battle. How do we change our mindsets—and how do we keep those changes alive over the long haul? This chapter aims to tackle these questions head-on by offering insights drawn from psychology, neuroscience, and real-world stories.

Before we explore the "how" for mindset changes, I want to remind you of the "why" to change our mindset. If you remember, in the introduction, we discussed a fixed mindset versus a growth mindset. As a review, a fixed mindset assumes that intelligence and abilities are static, you either have them, or you don't. This belief has led people to avoid challenges, resist feedback, and give up easily in the face of obstacles. In contrast, a growth mindset recognizes that skills and intelligence can be developed through effort, learning, and persistence. Those with a growth mindset embrace challenges as opportunities to grow, view effort as a path to mastery, and see failures as valuable learning experiences rather than personal shortcomings.

I have shared numerous stories and examples of how GenAI changes everything around us. If we have a fixed mindset and refuse to embrace this technology or tell ourselves we can't learn it, we risk living in a world that evolves without us. You don't want to be like a fax machine at a high-tech startup—functional, perhaps, but painfully outdated and irrelevant. Changing your mindset about AI isn't just a personal preference, it's a professional necessity. But while changing can feel intimidating, it can also spark excitement: we are, quite literally, on the cusp of rewiring how we learn, collaborate, and create.

I want to repeat that last part more forcefully...AI can be fun! It is the easiest technology to use in the history of the world. You can use GenAI technology by simple typing or even speaking. To help you develop a growth mindset, I will turn to several principles discovered by neuropsychology.

The first principle is neuroplasticity. This is a big fancy word that means our brains can rewire and adapt based on new experiences, learning, and repeated behaviors. In simple terms, your brain is not fixed. Your brain is more like a muscle that grows stronger the more you challenge it. When you try new things, like learning an AI tool, your brain creates and strengthens neural connections, making it easier over time. Although this is easier for young people, it also holds true for older people. This means that even if AI feels intimidating now, with consistent exposure and practice, your brain will adapt and improve.

Research shows that even being taught about neuroplasticity can improve your learning. Individuals who are trained to believe in a growth mindset show minor improvements in academic performance and larger improvements in mental health (e.g., reductions in stress, anxiety, and depression). To adopt the right AI mindset, start by believing you can grow and succeed with this technology.

The second principle we learn from neuropsychology is about fear. One major barrier to changing our mindset is fear: fear of looking silly, fear of losing a job, fear of an "AI apocalypse." Research on our brains shows that this fear response originates in the amygdala, an ancient part of our brain that screams, "Danger!" whenever we sense uncertainty. The amygdala is a small, almond-shaped structure in our brain that plays a large role in processing emotions, fear, and survival instincts. When we feel the fight or flight response, that is our amygdala speaking, usually screaming at us to do something.

Luckily, research has shown that another part of our brain can override the amygdala. This is our prefrontal cortex. The prefrontal cortex is the rational, decision-making part of our brain. It allows us to regulate emotions, plan, focus, and problem solve. The prefrontal cortex can override that impulse through higher reasoning. For instance, when you start to feel fear because of AI, you can ask yourself, "Is this fear realistic? What evidence do I have that my fears are true?" By asking those, or similar questions, the prefrontal cortex dampens the amygdala's alarm bells. Over time, repeated calm engagement with what used to scare us—like new AI technologies—teaches the amygdala that the "threat" is manageable.

You can even use AI to help manage fear and anxiety about the technology itself. Open a GenAI tool and explain your situation. For instance, you might say, "Hey ChatGPT, I'm struggling with fear about GenAI taking my job as a professor. I want you to help me reason through this in a positive way so I can have a rational, realistic response to the threat of GenAI on my job." You can then have a conversation and think about your fears. Realize some of your fears may be justified, but others may not be. However, by making sure you are not processing only with your amygdala, you will be in a better position to make a good decision.

The third relevant principle from neuropsychology is cognitive flexibility, which is your brain's ability to adapt, shift perspectives, and adjust to new information. In an AI-driven world, cognitive flexibility is more important than ever because technology constantly evolves. The ability to quickly learn, unlearn, and relearn is what separates those who thrive from those who feel left behind.

Cognitive flexibility allows you to break free from rigid thinking patterns. It enables you to pivot when AI changes the way tasks are done, rather than resisting or clinging to outdated methods. For example, when spreadsheets were first introduced, many accountants resisted, preferring to stick with paper ledgers. But those who embraced the new tools became more efficient, accurate, and valuable.

One simple way to improve cognitive flexibility is to intentionally expose yourself to new tools, tasks, or experiences. If AI intimidates you, start small. Play with a chatbot, ask it to rewrite a funny joke, or use an AI image generator to create something silly. The goal is to engage without pressure, proving to your brain that AI is not a threat but an opportunity. You can then build from small experiments to more meaningful applications, such as trying something at work.

Another powerful tool is reframing challenges as opportunities. Instead of thinking, "AI is making my job harder," train yourself to ask, "How can I use AI to make my job easier?" Your cognitive flexibility will improve if you develop the habit of questioning your first reaction and considering alternative viewpoints. This will help you navigate AI advancements with curiosity rather than fear.

Finally, cognitive flexibility thrives on lifelong learning. Commit to continuously expanding your AI knowledge, even if it's just a little bit at a time. Whether that means watching tutorials, attending workshops, or asking AI itself to explain unfamiliar concepts, the more you engage, the easier it will be to adapt to the AI revolution instead of being left behind by it.

The three cognitive principles of neuroplasticity, over-ruling your amygdala, and cognitive flexibility can be combined with more traditional behavioral mechanisms to help you change your mindsets. Will Durant, an American historian and philosopher, summarized many of Aristotle's ideas when he said, "We are what we repeatedly do. Excellence, then, is not an act, but a habit." This holds true with GenAI.

The two biggest mistakes I see individuals and organizations make are not trying AI at all—or giving up too soon.

Related to the first mistake, I was on an academic committee that was trying to develop a policy around AI usage for research. It was surprising how strong a negative opinion some academics had about this technology. What was even more surprising as we discussed it was that many of those with the most negative opinions had never even tried using it or had used it very sparingly. The advice in Dr. Seuss's *Green Eggs and Ham* is best in these situations (adapted with the help of ChatGPT):

```
You do not like AI, you say?
You will not try it? Not today?
You shake your head, you cross your arms,
You think it's full of risks and harms.
But have you tried it? Have you seen?
Have you asked it things unseen?
Just one small prompt, just one quick test,
```

```
You might just find it's not a pest!
Try it once and you may see,
It's not as scary as can be.
Try it here or try it there,
Try it, try it anywhere!
Try it once, just give it play—
You might just like AI one day!
```

The second mistake is trying ChatGPT and then dismissing it too quickly. As noted by Durrant and Aristotle, excellence comes from repetition, or "practice makes permanent." Each of us has set up routines in our lives that make it easy to go from day to day. Without effort, we will continually fall back into those routines, and any change will be difficult to make permanent. The same holds true for GenAI usage. Here are some practical ways to make sure you can continue with your initial attempts to incorporate AI into your life.

The first suggestion is to set up an accountability group. Find a few coworkers who want to learn about GenAI and make a deal that you will meet each week over lunch to discuss one thing that worked with GenAI and one thing you tried that didn't work. Seeing the strengths and weaknesses of GenAI will enable you to avoid early burnout when you have a string of failures. The accountability of the group will help force you to keep trying. It will also help you learn from others. This can enhance cognitive flexibility because you can see many ways to use the technology. If you want to speed up your adoption, make a goal to share with a friend each day a success and failure. This could be shared via email or a shared document so you can compile a list of successes and failures.

You'll find that after a few weeks of this, you will have a very long list of ideas of how you and the rest of the people in your organization can successfully use GenAI and a list of things you should avoid doing. More importantly, you'll have established a habit of experimenting with the technology, which will decrease fear-inducing amygdala responses. With the "hard facts" of what GenAI can do and not do, you will know how to position yourself for the future to continue adding value and not be replaced by the technology.

As you create this list of things that AI can't do, it is also worth periodically returning to the list of things AI can't do as new versions come out. With AI rapidly changing over time, you will find that some of the things AI couldn't do in the past it can do with future development. That is why when I'm asked in workshops, "Can AI do...<fill in the blank>?" I always answer "Yes" or "Not yet."

These group meetings shouldn't just be AI "puffery." The goal is to become a wise user of technology and know what is possible and what is not. Challenge your colleagues and invite them to challenge you. These sharing sessions aim not to have the right answer but to learn the right process. You'll need to shift your fixed mindset rooted in rigid rules to a growth mindset that embraces how both the technology and your use of it is evolving.

There are additional ways to sustain your development with GenAI. A stronger form of the co-worker group idea is to make a public commitment. There are various ways you can do this, but you might consider joining or starting a social media community, such as a LinkedIn group, where you commit to sharing once a week something you have learned or done from your own experimentation with GenAI and one thing you have learned from reading what others have done with GenAI. Public commitment is a stronger form of commitment; it also has the potential to open you to learning from a more diverse audience than your co-worker network.

As an additional possibility, consider "habit stacking" as you work to incorporate your new AI mindsets. Habit stacking is where you take an existing habit and pair it with a new one, making it easier to integrate into your daily routine. For example, if you already start your day by reading industry news, you could add a quick experiment with GenAI—perhaps using it to summarize articles or generate insights.

One way I habit stack my use of GenAI is when I come into the office in the morning, I open my email, and then I open a ChatGPT window. I have a three-screen monitor and so on one screen my email is open, and on another, I keep ChatGPT open. In this way, I have a constant visual reminder to use the tool throughout my day.

These are a few ideas. Can you think of more? If you can't, I hope you immediately had the thought, "I wonder if AI could help me brainstorm more ideas?" If you had that thought, you are on your way to changing your mindset about how GenAI can help you.

CHAPTER 12

Managing AI and Humans: The New Leadership Challenge

I sat in a presentation by an AI leader of one of the four largest accounting firms in the world. The speaker stunned me with a prediction, he stated, "Your students will need to graduate prepared to lead a team of PhDs on their first day of work." This statement contrasts drastically with the current mentorship model of these large accounting firms. Pre-AI, a typical student would be an intern, focusing on learning the basics and handling entry-level tasks. As they gained experience, they would become staff accountants, developing technical expertise and efficiency. Leadership opportunities typically began at the senior level, where they would start overseeing interns and newer staff, reviewing work, and providing guidance. As managers, they would take on greater leadership by directing entire teams, managing client relationships, and ensuring project success. At the senior manager and partner levels, they would lead multiple teams, set strategic direction, and influence firm-wide decisions. Compared to the historical progression, this speaker suggested a drastically different world that would require a completely different mindset.

What did the speaker mean? Current GenAI technology has the knowledge equal to or superior to most human PhDs...in every discipline. Companies are increasingly deploying GenAI solutions to perform various tasks, particularly through agents, as we discussed in a previous chapter. The concept of a team is no longer just made up of humans, but humans and agents (remember our discussion of Symbio?). Thus, a new hire would be unlikely to lead a human team on day one but will likely lead a team of AI agents on day one.

As this example demonstrates, leadership in the age of AI will look different in several ways than it currently does. Here are a few changes. You will be leading at a younger age. On almost every team you lead, someone will know more than you about everything. The smartest member of the team, the AI, will also have the least ego, as it will simply do whatever you ask. The egoless AI team members will not play any office politics, get upset if you say something wrong, or try to sabotage your project to jump you in line for promotion. The AI team members will also be able to work 24 hours a day without fatigue. You will have the hard job of thinking of ways to keep the AI team members busy.

The brilliant AI team members may also be incredibly dumb at times and not be able to perform simple tasks. You might explain something, only for the AI to misinterpret it in overly simplistic ways, making a mess of a project. I'm reminded of the children's books about Amelia Bedelia. Amelia Bedelia is a well-meaning housekeeper who takes every instruction literally, leading to humorous misunderstandings—like when she's told to "draw the curtains" and sketches them with a pencil.

AI can make the same kinds of mistakes in a business context. You might ask an AI to "streamline expense reports," expecting it to organize and analyze spending, but instead, it deletes every line item under $10 to "streamline" the data. The AI technically followed instructions, but not in the way you intended. As a leader, you will have to figure out how to work with a brilliant Ph.D. who can also be clueless.

Now, add complexity of human coworkers to the challenge of working with AI team members. One of your team members may quickly master how to get the best results from AI, drastically increasing his productivity. Meanwhile, others—Luddites (historically, workers who resisted industrial automation)—may refuse to even try AI, creating frustration and a growing skills gap within the team. As a leader, you won't just be managing AI mistakes, you'll also be navigating the widening divide between those who embrace AI and those who resist it.

With that backdrop, I want to suggest several mindset shifts to help you be a more successful leader in the AI world. I will group these mindset shifts by principles that are not new but are now more important, including humility, emotional intelligence, communication, adaptability, and vision.

Let's start with the most difficult and most important principle: humility. In a typical team, we appoint the "best" person to be the leader. We often define best by the person with the most experience, who is the smartest, or who has the most talent. As we have already demonstrated, it will be increasingly unlikely that you will ever be the "best" person in a group as the AI will be smarter and can work harder than you in any group you belong to. Recognizing that takes a big dose of humility and a change in how you lead.

One of the first things you must change is the idea that you are the smartest person in the room as the leader to recognize you are now "orchestrating intelligence." This phrase is perfect as an orchestra provides a great example of what this looks like. The conductor at a symphony is likely not better than any of the musicians she is leading at playing their individual instruments. Yet, she can be highly successful at directing her "team." Her competitive advantage comes not in being the best at each individual part, but instead in getting all the musicians to play together and accentuate each of their strengths at the right time.

To do this, the conductor must not only have humility herself, but she must be able to help inspire humility in each musician. Imagine creating an orchestra of the very best human musicians of all time, which is what AI teams will look like in the future. Each one of these musicians has the talent to be the star of the show, yet some will have to play the inglorious third string notes to make the overall performance succeed. Now, the leader in the AI world will not have a problem telling an AI to play third string, but what about telling the human, or the human and AI, that they must play third string in the group when the human thinks they should be the star? This will be even harder if the person has 30 years of experience and was once the company's top performer in the pre-AI world.

To be successful, this humility-based leadership mindset will require the leader to move away from authority-based leadership to influence-based leadership. To lead through influence rather than authority, leaders must refine their skills that foster collaboration, trust, and a shared sense of purpose. In the AI era, where knowledge and expertise are widely distributed—both among humans and AI systems—command-and-control leadership structures will become less successful. Instead, leaders will need to persuade, guide, and empower their teams, rather than dictate orders from a position of assumed superiority.

These examples show that closely related to humility is emotional intelligence. Emotional intelligence is the capacity to recognize, understand, manage, and effectively utilize emotions in oneself and others. At its core, AI is an algorithm that is not capable of emotion, although it could be programmed to act like it has emotion. Paradoxically, working with a non-emotional entity will require leaders to have greater emotional intelligence. Emotional intelligence is not geared towards the AI but towards the rest of the humans you will be working with.

As teams will be made up of more AI and humans working together, the importance of managing human emotions will be magnified. We have already discussed ego, but there will be many other emotions to manage. Think of the following situations and the emotions that will be present (I list some of the emotions in parentheses):

- An employee particularly adept at working with AI can produce twice the output in half the time as other team members. *(Pride, frustration, jealousy, inadequacy)*

- A long-time employee struggles to adapt to AI tools and fears being replaced by automation. *(Anxiety, insecurity, resistance, frustration)*

- A manager is forced to choose between investing in AI-powered solutions that increase efficiency or retaining employees whose jobs may become obsolete. *(Ethical dilemma, guilt, concern, apprehension)*

- A junior team member quickly learns AI skills and begins outperforming their more experienced colleagues. *(Excitement, resentment, motivation, insecurity)*

- A team must collaborate with an AI-driven system that occasionally makes mistakes, leading to confusion and miscommunication. *(Frustration, doubt, skepticism, problem-solving drive)*

- An AI system detects patterns and recommends a decision that contradicts human intuition, creating tension between tech-savvy and traditional employees. *(Uncertainty, distrust, curiosity, determination)*

- A leader must mediate a conflict between employees who feel threatened by AI and those who embrace it. *(Frustration, fear, optimism, defensiveness)*

- An AI-assisted hiring process recommends candidates that differ from what human recruiters would have chosen, leading to internal disagreements. *(Skepticism, bias, hesitation, curiosity)*

- An AI model makes a mistake that negatively impacts a customer, requiring a human employee to step in and repair the relationship. *(Embarrassment, responsibility, empathy, accountability)*

Those examples largely focus on negative emotions, but there are potential positive situations as well:

- An employee collaborates with AI to create a breakthrough innovation, receiving company-wide recognition for their efforts. *(Excitement, pride, validation, inspiration)*

- An AI-powered system helps a remote team coordinate across time zones, improving efficiency and work-life balance. *(Convenience, relief, harmony, gratitude)*

- A workplace competition challenges employees to find creative AI applications, leading to friendly rivalry and innovation. (*Engagement, excitement, teamwork, curiosity*)

- An AI-generated analysis helps a sales team identify new customer trends, leading to record-breaking revenue growth. (*Confidence, celebration, pride, enthusiasm*)

- AI-driven automation reduces stress by predicting peak workloads and reallocating resources accordingly. (*Calmness, control, reassurance, trust*)

- A leader uses AI-powered insights to identify employee strengths, enabling better career growth and personal development opportunities. (*Fulfillment, confidence, empowerment, gratitude*)

- AI helps HR match employees with projects that align with their skills and passions, increasing job satisfaction. (*Excitement, fulfillment, engagement, happiness*)

- An AI tool translates real-time conversations, allowing employees from different countries to communicate effortlessly, fostering inclusiveness. (*Connection, cultural appreciation, belonging, unity*)

All these situations will require emotional intelligence. I focus on two situations that leaders will face, posing them as questions for you to think about what you would do. I expect the first to relate to things we saw with work-from-home initiatives that accelerated because of the COVID-19 pandemic. The pandemic required many employees to work from home. This has both challenges and opportunities. One challenge leaders had to address was how to help team members have connections and create community. In the AI world, there will be increasing amounts of time working with less human interaction and more machine interaction. Leaders will have to find ways to foster human connection when there is less human interaction. How will you do that?

The second challenge is what happens with increased productivity. At first glance, this is an easy decision. If all your employees are 15% more productive, everyone will make more money and everyone will be happier. While that sounds nice, it is much more complex than that. Many employees who create value are on salary, and increased productivity doesn't change any of the benefits they receive. In fact, increased productivity will only mean they have to do more work. While some of the drudgery will hopefully be eliminated from their job, they will likely have more stress from having to complete more projects, or projects that require more focus. The leader in the AI world will have to figure out how to keep their employees from burning out because of increased demands from increased productivity. There will be difficult questions such as deciding who gets the rewards from the productivity gains, whether those gains come in the form of increased compensation or additional free time. As a leader, are you prepared to answer the question of who benefits from AI?

That will take emotional intelligence to reach a conclusion that all are happy with.

Building off emotional intelligence is the competency of communication. It is again ironic that employing more team members who just do what you say will require greater communication skills by leaders. The first type of improved communication is that leaders and their employees must learn how to communicate correctly with AI team members. That can be figured out with practice and training, but an under-appreciated aspect of this communication is the one-way nature of communication with AI. AI can be programmed to give feedback but doesn't communicate back like a human. You can't ask the AI team member, "Did that feel right?" nor can you expect it to always recognize when a message is too harsh, too vague, or might be misinterpreted by a human colleague.

Similarly, AI lacks the ability to interpret subtle social dynamics, such as detecting sarcasm or understanding unspoken tensions in a conversation. It's not (yet) going to see, let alone interpret, an eye roll, a heavy sigh, or other nonverbal communication that a human will give. Another challenge is that AI doesn't build rapport or trust in the same way humans do—while it can remember preferences and personalize responses, it doesn't genuinely care about a colleague's well-being or motivation. These gaps in human-like communication mean leaders must develop new skills to effectively integrate AI into their teams.

Leaders will also have to figure out how to communicate with their team members about AI team members. When something goes wrong because of an AI, who is held accountable? Is it the AI's fault or the humans fault for not catching the mistake? Setting clear expectations and communicating the expectations will be important to keep everyone moving forward.

The next principle is adaptability. I was part of a roundtable discussion with the entire finance function of one of the top ten largest companies in the world. After the discussion, I visited with the chief accounting officer and he said he was going to start a planning meeting with his executives for the next five years. I asked him, "How in the world do you plan for five years ahead with things changing so fast?" He honestly responded, "I don't know."

In accounting, we used to joke about how hard it was to teach tax classes because every year the content changed. I chuckle about that now. This last semester, I was preparing to teach my technology class, which would start with teaching about GenAI. Two weeks before the start of my class, OpenAI had a "12 days of OpenAI," where they announced 12 new products or AI abilities. I updated my class to incorporate the relevant abilities. We then started the semester and finished talking about GenAI, and I told the students that I would update them at the end of the semester on any new GenAI developments. *During that lecture*, OpenAI released their Operator AI agent that could independently control web browsers, and within a week, they released the o3-mini models and deep reasoning capabilities. I can barely keep up with the pace of change in teaching, I can only imagine how hard it is for companies to keep up.

Whether in business or the classroom, adaptability in the AI era is not just about reacting to change—it's about being prepared for continuous transformation. The pace at which AI is evolving means that what is cutting-edge today may be outdated in months if not weeks. Leaders can no longer rely on static strategies or long-term roadmaps that assume stability. Instead, adaptability requires embracing a mindset of ongoing learning, rapid iteration, and a willingness to experiment. Organizations that wait for AI technologies to mature before integrating them may find themselves perpetually behind. In contrast, those that adopt an agile approach—testing and refining AI implementations in real time—will be the ones that stay ahead. The most successful leaders will be those who remain flexible enough to adjust their strategies as AI capabilities shift rather than rigidly clinging to outdated processes.

So, how do leaders practically build adaptability into their approach to AI? First, they must develop a culture of iterative decision-making—implementing AI in strategic ways, gathering feedback, and refining its role. Second, leaders should focus on building teams that are comfortable with ambiguity and open to change, emphasizing continuous learning rather than mastery of any single tool. This means encouraging employees to regularly experiment with new AI functionalities and share insights across the organization, even if the relevance to their roles isn't immediately clear. Finally, adaptability requires a shift in leadership style—leaders must become facilitators of change rather than enforcers of structure. Instead of viewing AI as a fixed toolset, they must see it as an evolving partner that demands ongoing assessment and realignment.

These four principles, humility, emotional intelligence, communication, and adaptability, will all influence the vision a leader must be able to provide for others. Vision has always been a hallmark of great leadership, but it will be even more important in the AI-driven future. Here's how these four principles will work together to help a leader establish a vision to motivate and inspire others.

Leaders who embrace humility understand they no longer need to have all the answers themselves. Instead, their strength comes from recognizing and orchestrating the intelligence of both human and AI team members. This humility allows them to shape a vision that empowers their team, fostering an environment where ideas are welcomed regardless of whether they originate from humans or AI. Such a vision inspires trust, openness, and collaboration, essential qualities in the rapidly evolving AI landscape. At the same time, emotional intelligence becomes crucial because leaders must navigate the human reactions triggered by the integration of AI. Team members may experience a variety of emotions, including excitement, anxiety, skepticism, or resistance. Leaders who can empathize, understand these emotions, and respond thoughtfully will create a vision that resonates deeply and authentically with their teams. By acknowledging and addressing emotional dynamics, leaders help their teams see AI not as a threat but as a partner in achieving shared goals.

Effective communication ties these elements together. Clearly articulating a vision means going beyond simply stating goals. Leaders must thoughtfully describe how AI and human collaboration will unfold in their organization, clarifying roles and expectations. By communicating transparently, leaders can reduce ambiguity and align diverse team members—AI enthusiasts and skeptics alike—toward a common purpose. Excellent communication ensures everyone understands the vision's intent and value, enhancing commitment and minimizing misunderstandings.

Finally, adaptability ensures that the leader's vision remains flexible and relevant amid constant technological advancements. Leaders must continuously reassess and refine their vision, adapting quickly to shifts in AI capabilities, market conditions, or organizational needs. Rather than a rigid blueprint, their vision serves as a guiding principle, allowing for experimentation, rapid learning, and ongoing iteration. This dynamic approach helps teams remain resilient and forward focused, embracing change rather than resisting it.

When integrated, these principles enable leaders to craft a compelling, adaptable vision that inspires their teams, leverages the combined strengths of human and AI intelligence, and positions their organizations for lasting success in a rapidly evolving world.

Let's end this chapter with a real-world example. Toni Ruiz, CEO of Mango, a leading Spanish fashion retailer, has modernized his company by embracing generative AI to revolutionize how they create content. One notable initiative was the use of AI-generated digital models in campaigns for the teen line, "Sunset Dream." Instead of relying solely on traditional human models, Mango captured real photographs of their clothes and then used an internal AI platform to superimpose these images onto digital avatars. This move accelerated content production and helped Mango maintain a consistent aesthetic aligned with its brand values.

Under Ruiz's leadership, these innovative practices have dovetailed with Mango's broader digital transformation strategy. The brand reported record-breaking performance. By reducing the time and cost associated with traditional photo shoots, Mango was able to invest those savings in expanding its store network and enhancing its digital presence.

Ruiz's approach demonstrates the new paradigm in leadership: one where the role is less about being the smartest person in the room and more about orchestrating a diverse team of human talent and advanced AI systems. His focus on clear communication, continuous learning, and adaptability has allowed him to harness AI as a tool that augments creativity rather than replaces it. In doing so, Ruiz not only boosted Mango's operational efficiency but also set a compelling example for leaders facing the challenge of integrating AI into traditional business models.

Your Move:
The AI Era Has Begun

As I conclude this book, I want to thank you sincerely for joining me on this journey. Throughout these pages, I've shared insights on how we must adapt our mindsets to effectively navigate and thrive in an AI-driven world. Yet this book has not just been about mindset shifts in theory—it has been about applying them in practice. And nowhere was that more evident than in my experience writing this very book.

From the outset, writing this book became an exercise in embracing the very principles I've outlined. I want to share a behind-the-scenes look at how this book itself came together. I had ideas, but I engaged with AI as a co-creator rather than working alone. This was a conscious decision—an acknowledgment that AI could enhance my thinking, not replace it. I used AI to brainstorm, fact-check, refine language, and draft short segments, but every decision remained mine. This was a real-world test of the co-creation mindset—understanding that AI is most effective when it serves as a collaborator, not a stand-alone writer.

This iterative process also provided an immediate lesson in adaptability. I have spent much of my career writing, but this was the first time I had written so much with AI. It required a shift in how I approached writing itself—no longer a solitary process, but a dynamic exchange between human creativity and machine efficiency. Sometimes, AI provided surprising insights that pushed me to explore perspectives I hadn't previously considered. Other times, it confidently produced text that felt generic or off the mark, requiring me to refine or discard its output. I quickly learned that prompting AI is an art in itself—the quality of what I received depended largely on how I framed my requests. As discussed in earlier chapters, the ability to ask the right questions—to refine, iterate, and guide AI toward better results— is a critical skill.

Interestingly, AI also played a role in alleviating my creative insecurities. At times, I found myself asking the AI for reassurance—was this book making sense? Was it worth trying to write it? Was I explaining things clearly? Its responses were optimistic, which was both helpful and amusing. While readers may form their own opinions, the AI's confidence encouraged me to keep moving forward rather than getting bogged down in perfection. This reinforced another crucial mindset shift: progress matters more than perfection. AI allowed me to focus on momentum—getting ideas onto the page, refining them later, and not allowing self-doubt to stall creativity.

Yet, despite this robust collaboration, I recognize that the book is neither perfect nor complete. AI technology is continuously evolving, and the mindsets required to thrive alongside it must inevitably evolve as well. This book is not a final statement, but a starting point. Just as I emphasize the importance of lifelong learning in an AI world, I recognize that my own understanding will need to continually adapt. New breakthroughs, new challenges, and new ethical considerations will emerge, requiring an ongoing willingness to update and refine our perspectives.

Remarkably, the process of writing this book illustrated another critical point: productivity in an AI world is being redefined. Composing a full-length book primarily over five weekends— writing intensively on Friday evenings and Saturdays—was achievable only because of my partnership with AI. Without AI's assistance, maintaining this pace while still preserving quality would have been nearly impossible. The mindset shift here was profound: what we once believed was an upper limit of human productivity is no longer fixed. AI has shattered traditional constraints, enabling individuals to create and iterate at speeds that were once unimaginable. However, this raises an important caution: just because we can produce faster doesn't mean we should always do it. I plan to take a few weekends off from work to rest and reset!

This process was not without friction. There were numerous occasions when I disagreed with AI-generated suggestions or outputs. AI is often brilliant, but it is also unreliable. It would fabricate references, misunderstand nuance, and sometimes overcomplicate ideas that needed simplicity. I quickly learned that using AI well requires critical engagement, not passive acceptance. This ties back to a fundamental mindset I emphasized earlier: the balance of trust and skepticism. AI can be a powerful amplifier of knowledge but also requires vigilance. Blindly accepting AI's output is as dangerous as blindly rejecting them.

The key is knowing when to trust, when to question, and when to verify. This comes best from experience.

An enormous benefit of partnering with AI was solving the blank page problem. Traditionally, starting from scratch is the most daunting part of writing. With AI, I always had a conversational partner to bounce ideas off. I even spent time commuting to work to chat with AI about the book. I would share ideas, ask for critiques, and try to learn as much as I could. Whether refining a concept, developing arguments, or structuring chapters, the AI consistently provided a productive starting point. This wasn't just about efficiency—it was about creative flow. By eliminating hesitation, AI allowed me to focus on higher-order thinking, ensuring that my effort was spent on shaping arguments rather than wrestling with writer's block. This speaks to another critical mindset shift: co-creating with AI doesn't just save time; it enhances creativity by reducing cognitive friction.

Of course, co-creation with AI comes with challenges. For instance, it frequently hallucinated, confidently fabricating scholarly references, case studies, and examples. Consequently, I relied heavily on personal experience, rigorous independent research, and careful verification. This reinforced the importance of expertise—a topic I explored in an earlier chapter. AI may know more facts than any single human, but true expertise is about knowing how to apply, interpret, and validate knowledge.

AI can assist with analysis, but humans must still exercise judgment.

Despite the exciting speed at which AI enabled me to produce this book, I don't envision maintaining this pace indefinitely. Writing a book every five weekends is neither sustainable nor desirable for me. Rather, I plan to deliberately slow down, using AI to augment—not overwhelm—my natural creative rhythms. This aligns with the "more is less" paradox I discussed earlier. AI allows for extraordinary productivity, but if we prioritize quantity over depth, we risk losing meaning in the pursuit of speed.

It's unlikely I'll ever return to purely human-driven writing. My "Symbio" experience—the enriching process of human-AI co-creation—has fundamentally changed my relationship with writing. This newfound "superpower" enables me to achieve more creatively and intellectually than I could alone, providing ample reason to continue this collaborative practice. This is the future of expertise—not replacing human skill, but augmenting it.

Looking toward the future, I've even begun imagining how AI might revolutionize the very nature of book writing itself. I think back to my childhood of reading choose-your-own-adventure books. In these books, you read a page and then, on the bottom of the page, choose what action you wanted to have happen and then turn to the appropriate page that continued your chosen storyline. Could a future genre of "books" be an author providing prompts that a reader uses to start the conversation? The reader continues asking questions about that prompt until they feel ready to move to the next directed prompt. One of my colleagues at Brigham Young University tried something similar in her class. Rather than assign just a traditional textbook to read from, she gave the students the learning objectives and vocabulary they needed to understand before class, and the students could use the AI to teach themselves. While my choose-your-own-adventure AI book may not catch on, certainly, the future will be filled with new inventions that allow humans and AI to partner in exciting new ways.

Some might question whether a co-created book like this is genuinely "mine." I believe it absolutely is. This book reflects my personal journey, insights, and expertise. Far from being AI-generated spam, it represents a meaningful collaboration that deepened my own understanding and improved the final product. The true hallmark of successful AI collaboration, I've found, is when it enhances both the output and the creator. You can use this as a yardstick to measure your own use of AI.

> *If the AI is making you and the product better, you are using it correctly. If either you or the product you are producing is not better, you should refine how you are using AI.*

I recognize that not every author will embrace this collaborative approach—and that's perfectly fine. Creativity is deeply personal, often serving as an emotional outlet rather than a professional pursuit. As I discussed earlier in the book, I like scroll sawing. Much like my preference for traditional scroll saw woodworking over faster, more precise laser-cutting tools, authors may choose to selectively incorporate AI into their creative processes. For my academic and professional writing, I will definitely continue with co-creation. However, for personal projects and creative hobbies, I will continue to selectively balance human and AI-driven creativity, preserving mental health and creative authenticity.

Ultimately, adapting our mindsets to the AI era isn't about fully embracing or entirely rejecting technology—it's about consciously choosing how best to integrate it into our lives and careers. I hope this book has provided a starting point for your mindset shift, empowering you to engage meaningfully and effectively with AI now and in the future.

Index

accounting, 32, 33, 34, 52, 72, 73, 74, 75, 80, 81, 89, 104, 105, 107, 136, 141, 157, 167

adaptability, 19, 30, 31, 39, 103, 159, 167, 168, 169, 170, 171, 174

agent, 32, 34, 37, 72, 100, 101, 167

AI comprehension, 82

AI development, 12, 132

AI God: Portrait of Alan Turing, 11

AI tool, 30, 149, 164

AI world, 7, 15, 26, 41, 76, 84, 86, 99, 100, 103, 104, 107, 133, 139, 146, 159, 160, 165, 175

AI-designed, 75

AI-driven, 10, 11, 85, 88, 92, 93, 108, 109, 142, 145, 150, 162, 164, 169, 173, 179

AI-generated, 87, 88, 93, 108, 123, 132, 164, 171, 176, 178

algorithm, 11, 35, 40, 140, 161

algorithms, 11, 18, 21, 24, 98, 115, 143

Amazon, 10

Analyze, 86, 87, 88

Anderson, Dr. Lorin, 86

anthropology, 104

API, 32

Apply, 57, 86, 88

architecture, 63, 96, 104, 105

astronomy, 104

autonomous vehicles, 114, 119, 120, 121

Bach, Johann Sebastian, 66

Bannister, Roger, 65

Beethoven, Ludwig van, 66

Bing, 19

Bird, Larry, 5

Bloom's Taxonomy, 86

brainstorming, 29, 36, 39, 45, 75, 76, 135

Brigham Young University, 76, 178

calculators, 1, 2, 23, 61, 125

centaur, 99, 100

Certified Internal Auditor, 72

Certified Management Accountant, 72

Certified Public Accountant, 72

Chamberlain, Wilt, 5

chatbot, 19, 20, 21, 80, 82, 129, 151

ChatGPT, 7, 9, 12, 14, 19, 28, 35, 38, 46, 47, 51, 52, 55, 71, 72, 73, 80, 83, 105, 140, 150, 152, 153, 155

ChatGPT 3.5, 7, 9, 71, 72

ChatGPT 4, 9

chess, 97, 99, 106

CIA. See Certified Internal Auditor

cinematography, 104

Claude 3.5 Sonnet, 14
CMA. See Certified Management
  Accountant
co-creation, 39, 174, 177, 179
Connor Group, 92
contextual, 30
CoPilot, 19
COVID-19, 165
CPA. See Certified Public
  Accountant
Create, 55, 86, 87, 88
creativity, 11, 21, 23, 24, 29, 31,
  33, 34, 36, 39, 45, 46, 59, 62,
  64, 67, 74, 121, 147, 171, 174,
  175, 176, 179
critical thinking, 39, 94
culinary arts, 104
Curry, Stephen, 47, 48
cybersecurity, 104
DARPA. See Defense Advanced
  Research Projects Agency
Deep Blue, 97, 98, 99
deepfake, 135, 136, 137, 138
DeepSeek, 130
Defense Advanced Research
  Projects Agency, 114, 115, 120
deterministic, 18, 23, 24, 27, 28,
  32, 33, 34, 39, 40, 112, 122,
  133, 147
digital competency, 82
digital computing, 92
Disney, 10, 134
Durant, Will, 152
Dweck, Dr. Carol, 8
economics, 80, 104
Einstein, Albert, 96

emotional intelligence, 159, 161,
  164, 166, 169
Encyclopedia Britannica, 4
engineering, 69, 73, 92, 104, 138
environmental science, 104
ESPN, 47, 48
Eulerich, Marc, 72
European Union, 12
Evaluate, 86, 87, 88
EY Academic Resource Center,
  74
EYARC. See EY Academic
  Resource Center
Facebook, 4
fashion, 6, 104, 171
Gatsby, Jay, 142
Gemini, 19, 129
GenAI, 11, 12, 14, 19, 20, 21, 22,
  23, 26, 27, 28, 29, 30, 31, 32,
  33, 34, 35, 36, 37, 38, 39, 40,
  41, 42, 43, 44, 45, 46, 48, 49,
  50, 52, 53, 55, 59, 60, 62, 63,
  64, 71, 74, 75, 76, 77, 80, 81,
  82, 83, 87, 88, 89, 90, 91, 93,
  94, 97, 104, 108, 109, 111,
  112, 113, 114, 120, 121, 122,
  123, 128, 130, 132, 133, 134,
  135, 138, 139, 140, 145, 146,
  148, 150, 152, 153, 154, 155,
  158, 167
genetics, 104
Golden State Warriors, 47
Google, 2, 19, 25, 35, 41, 42, 43,
  44, 45, 47, 48, 55, 129
graphic design, 104
Great Depression, 4

Grok-2, 14
hallucinations, 35, 36, 37, 38, 39,
    133, 134, 135, 145
Hedonic Treadmill, 142, 145
history, 4, 5, 66, 68, 92, 97, 99,
    101, 104, 108, 114, 116, 129,
    148
HLE. See Humanities Last Exam
human decisions, 122, 125, 132
human expertise, 92, 94, 147
Humanities Last Exam, 13
human-ness, 61
IBM, 3, 97, 98
Imagen 3, 55
Internet, 2, 9, 22, 24, 41, 46, 47,
    140
InvestAI, 12
jagged technological frontier, 69,
    70, 71, 76, 112
James, LeBron, 5
Japan, 42, 43
Jassy, Andy, 10
Johnson, Magic, 5
Jordan, Michael, 5
Kasparov, Gary, 97
Kennedy, John F., 4
Krathwohl, Dr. David, 86
Large Language Models, 21, 25
law, 2, 3, 7, 35, 41, 104
lawyer, 35, 38, 39
linguistics, 104
literature, 88, 104, 128, 142
LLMs. See Large Language
    Models
long-distance phone calls, 2, 7
Mango, 171

Manhattan Project, 96
math, 12, 18, 30, 31, 35, 36, 46,
    89, 91, 103, 104
MATH dataset, 12
McCain, John, 4
medicine, 5, 104
meteorology, 104
mindset, 2, 4, 5, 6, 7, 8, 9, 15, 21,
    27, 28, 29, 31, 33, 36, 38, 39,
    40, 41, 42, 45, 48, 52, 53, 54,
    61, 62, 63, 65, 66, 73, 84, 89,
    91, 92, 93, 97, 104, 105, 107,
    111, 112, 114, 118, 120, 121,
    122, 123, 130, 131, 132, 133,
    134, 139, 140, 141, 143, 145,
    146, 147, 148, 149, 154, 155,
    158, 159, 161, 168, 173, 174,
    175, 176, 179
model, 12, 14, 21, 22, 23, 24, 25,
    26, 29, 37, 46, 55, 72, 73, 88,
    112, 127, 128, 129, 130, 131,
    136, 137, 157, 163
Mollick, Ethan, 69
more is less, 141, 143, 145, 177
Mozart, 67
music, 6, 26, 66, 67, 68, 76, 85,
    104
NASA, 92, 93
NBA, 5
Neumann, John von, 95
new AI world, 7, 133
Nokia, 3
Obama, Barack, 4
OpenAI, 7, 12, 19, 25, 72, 167
Oracle, 12
Perfect is the enemy of good, 111

perfectionist, 111, 112, 116, 118, 120, 121, 123
philosophy, 104
physics, 20, 104
Pikoos, Jason, 92, 94
political science, 104
probabilistic, 23, 27, 28, 29, 30, 33, 34, 35, 36, 39, 40, 111, 122, 133, 147
Procter & Gamble, 102
prompt. See
psychology, 79, 80, 104, 147
psychometrics, 79
Remember, 40, 71, 86, 87, 106, 111
responsibility, 38, 39, 163
Reuters, 47
rise of AI, 7
robotics, 104
Roosevelt, Franklin D., 4
Ruiz, Toni, 171
Sanatizadeh, Aida, 72
science fiction, 31
SEC. See Securities and Exchange Commission
Securities and Exchange Commission, 137
SoftBank, 12
SQL, 89, 90

StageCraft, 10
strawberry, 34
Studebaker, 4
Suno.AI, 67, 68
Symbio, 100, 101, 103, 104, 105, 107, 108, 158, 177
taking jobs away, 32
taxonomy, 86
tech breaks, 145
Teller, Edward, 96
temperature, 23, 24, 27
tensors, 22, 24
The Mandalorian, 10
theology, 104
tokens, 22, 23, 24, 34
Turing, Alan, 11
Twitter, 4
Understand, 86, 87
user preferences, 30
Vakilzadeh, Hamid, 72
vigilance, 39, 146, 176
virtual private network, 10
visualization, 93
VPN. See virtual private network
Wigner, Eugene, 96
Wikipedia, 4
World Bank, 81
X, 4, 19, 112